"What I really like about Accelerate Personal Performance is the combination of storytelling and practical ideas. There are no 'hacks' or sugarcoating the hard work that is required to succeed but rather a big dollop of encouraging realism."

Debra Searle MVO MBE, Solo Atlantic Rower

"Ralph Varcoe has packed this book with tips and stories that will inspire you to achieve success - in whatever field you choose."

Paul Sloane, best selling author

"If you're looking to achieve the goals you've always wanted and need that little nudge of inspiration and sound advice, then this entertaining and thought-provoking book is for you."

Howard Ford, Chairman Pyreos Ltd & Displaydata Ltd

"Great storytelling mixed with science make this an amazing book for everyone looking for that little bit extra to push them to achieve their best. Love it."

Pete Pastides, Managing Partner Intelligence Partners

———————◇———————

Also by Ral

60 Ways t

ISBN: 978-1-78972-628-2

ACCELERATE PERSONAL PERFORMANCE

RALPH VARCOE

For E, P, A, C, and M.

From 'This girl can' to 'These girls do', Accelerated.

CONTENTS

ACKNOWLEDGMENTS

This book has been a joy to research and write. I've learned so much from so many people and I'm truly grateful to them all. From the experts in their fields to great sporting heroes who continue to inspire. And above all the people I've worked with over the years who I mention in the (mostly) anonymised stories I tell.

1. INTRODUCTION

The Problem

At the end of every Sunday Sally would get the usual Sunday evening blues. The weekend had slipped past, and she'd achieved nothing very much. She knew it was right when people told her that weekends are for recharging your batteries, but still, she hadn't done half the things she wanted to do. The blog she had started with such enthusiasm only a matter of three weeks ago hadn't been touched since then. Somehow, she just didn't know what to write about next. The house was still in a mess, and the guest bedroom wasn't going to paint itself, and she didn't see why she should pay someone to do a half-decent job when painting really isn't that hard.

On the plus side, Sally had seen two of her friends. One was an old school friend who she used to be close to about 22 years ago. They'd met for a coffee at John Lewis, but somehow that had turned into a shopping spree for things she didn't need, and then lunch. She'd got home three hours later than she'd planned, with shopping bags full of clothes and stuff for the house, and a purse that was considerably lighter. She'd felt a little sick that she'd spent money she was supposed to be saving for her three-month travels and had wasted a few unscheduled hours. Was it fair to call them wasted? She had enjoyed herself, but she'd planned to get a lot more done, all of which had fallen by the wayside.

Another had been her Saturday evening going out buddy. They had been friends for years, and when there was nothing else happening, they'd meet up for a few drinks and a laugh. Only it seemed that every time they met up, she had rather more to drink than she'd planned. Yet more money, and a tipsy taxi ride home to be greeted by the cat's surly expression at 1.30 in the morning, followed by a night of fitful sleep, and sore head in the morning. Consequently, Sunday morning had been a slow affair.

By lunchtime, Sally was feeling a little more normal, so decided to tackle the garden, slowly. A couple of hours and a few cups of tea later, and there had been a pile of dying weeds lying on the flagstones, and a garden that looked pretty much the same as it had done before she'd started. As the evening settled in, she was getting 'that' feeling again -work in the morning, and her life given over for the next five days to her employer. She quite liked her job, and her boss was actually rather good to work for, but somehow, every weekend without fail, she would end feeling like this. Perhaps it was learned from school days.

To add to the normal blues feeling, Sally had beaten herself up over her failings. She had seen all the things she hadn't done as big, bright failures. Flashing neon signs that had followed her to bed, and that had still been there in the morning.

"Next weekend", she had said to herself as she showered and readied herself for the day and week ahead.

How many times have you wished there were more hours in the day? That you could get a few more things done?

The problem is that life gets in the way. It is so easy to be distracted from what you want to do. The annoying dripping tap that needs a washer changing. The email from eBay saying your account has been locked because they think someone other than you placed something for sale last night when it had been you all along. And the biggest culprit of them all, Le Grand Fromage of time-wasting, Facebook was just that little bit more appealing than the assignment, household bills, letter you were going to write, or some work. Then there is the critical match or Grand Prix on TV, or Game of Thrones is about to start.

Some of those are just annoying time wasters. Others are enjoyable but are also time wasters, nevertheless. The point is that they are all distractions from what you might want to achieve.

This book is for people who know they have more to offer, either at home, personally, or at work, and who want to understand how to accelerate their performance. The fact is that most things are hard to do. You may have an aptitude for playing a musical instrument but to become exceptional takes a lot of hard work. In 'Outliers: The story of success', Malcolm Gladwell famously states that what's required to become a master of a skill is 10,000 hours of deliberate practice. That is the equivalent of spending 24 hours a day, every day for 1.15 years, or 14 months, or 417 days straight.

Many people shy away from much dedicated hard work, but it is only through hard work and dedication that they achieve their best. Usain Bolt, Richard Branson, Larry Ellison, Bill Gates, David Beckham, and Johnny Wilkinson achieved greatness by working hard. Beckham could place a free-kick where he wanted it to go because he spent hour, upon hour practising. Johnny Wilkinson would spend extra hours place-kicking so that he could become the World Cup winner for England in 2003. Bill Gates, Larry Ellison, and Richard Branson work harder than I do, and probably many of you too.

But more than hard work, they had a passion for it, as without passion for reaching goals, hard work results in burn out. Bill Gates makes a great comment in a televised conversation with his father that you don't get to 10,000 hours unless you have fanatical passion. Something just kept him and his cohort going. The fire was continuously stoked as they saw success, as they had fun, as they grew. So how do you get some passion of your own?

Accelerate Personal Performance will help you take the first steps towards achieving your goals. The aim is to help you accelerate your performance, in whatever area that happens to be. Over the next couple of hundred pages, we'll look at science, common sense and stories of greatness. Take from them what you want so that you can put in place your own plan to accelerate your performance.

If you are stuck, moving nowhere towards your goal, then this book will help you accelerate from 0-60mph.

If you are moving towards your goal, but it's just a little slower than you'd like, then we'll get you from 60-100mph.

After 100mph, your momentum will keep you going, but the lessons in this book will help refresh you and enable you to keep your foot on the accelerator.

Authority? What Authority?

As I leant up against the window of the reception desk, watching the world go by outside the Fulham Pools, I sighed a heavy sigh.

"No-one is heading this way", I huffed to Martin who was shuffling paper behind the counter.

"Aye, it's cold and dark", he helpfully pointed out. "These Southerners hide indoors when it gets below about six degrees. We hard nuts from north of the border swim in any weather. I've been windsurfing on the North Sea when it's been freezing before now."

How helpful, I thought. I was doomed to selling no memberships because it was winter, and all of us who lived in London were 'soft Southerners' according to Martin.

"I've got to do something to relieve my boredom", I moaned. "Maybe organise a jazz concert again".

"Good idea", Martin lilted sarcastically. "What exactly do you know about music then?"

"Well, before I took this meaningless, godforsaken job, I was a musician. I studied singing at the Guildhall. Classical mainly, but I also sing some jazz with a mate. We were on 'Loose Ends' once."

"You learn something new every day. So why did you take this job."

"Needed the cash. A musician's life is one suffered for the sake of art", I enunciated theatrically.

"You don't have to sell memberships here, OR be a musician", Martin suggested. "Why not be both?"

"I suppose I could", I sighed back. "But I don't feel motivated to do anything much."

Martin paused, then stated emphatically, "Doing doesn't come from motivation. Rather, motivation comes from doing."

At that moment, a lightbulb flashed in my head.

That's a true story. I did attend the Guildhall and thought that I wanted to be a professional baritone, just as my uncle had been. Music was the family business — grandmother, father, uncle and sister. But somehow its draw wasn't quite enough to keep me away from so many other things. After I quit the Guildhall, I studied homoeopathy for three years. I discovered that homoeopathy just wasn't for me.

Listless periods of drifting into the next thing that could keep the wolf from the door were frequent after that. Teaching English to speakers of other languages was one such flirtation. All I learned was that most foreigners had a better grasp of English grammar than I did, which considering I was supposed to be teaching it was a little sad. I didn't last long.

The Fulham pools were a friendly and warm place to hang out every day, and it wasn't difficult selling memberships to those that thought they'd swim more than twice a week. It didn't pay very well, but at least it was a job, and I had stopped costing my parents their hard-earned teachers' savings. It was there I met Martin, and even though he usually is quite dour, he occasionally said some rather insightful things.

I picked up the phone and booked a venue in Ealing for three consecutive nights in April. As I read out my credit card number over the phone, I closed my eyes tightly and tried to block out all thoughts. I had just agreed to spend a month's pay on a venue for three months hence. Holy crap!

I can attest to the fact that Martin was right. Suddenly I had things to do, lots of them — rehearsals, programmes, tickets, advertising, grand piano hire, sound equipment, lighting, songwriting, panicking. The shows went better than I could have hoped for — lots of bums on seats, and applause. And I broke even — what a relief.

That success prompted me to organise a recording, and a few months later a CD was made which we sold at concerts (also available on Amazon and iTunes).

From then on, I moved from being listless to being a list king. Everything was on a list somewhere. Actions resulted in progress and created more activities until eventually each written down goal was crossed off the list. I networked my way to a job in software sales in a small company, then on to a small telecoms company, followed by a global player. Not content with being a junior account executive, I drove onwards and became a VP of sales within a few years. As my career progressed pretty fast, I felt I wanted to acquire some skills, knowledge, and insights along the way, so enrolled in an MBA at Henley Business School.

Arranged in learning groups for the three-year part-time course, I found myself amongst a group of very like-minded people. Everyone was from a different background, but three of the team, in particular, shared my goal to finish the course within the scheduled time, or earlier. That doesn't sound too difficult until you realise that 40% of those that enrol never complete the course at all, and of the rest, 95% of them finish late, some of them years late. I was determined to finish on time.

I sold my boat – my pride and joy – sailing is a big passion of mine. I knew I would need no distractions for three years. I knew it would be bloody hard to complete the course, pass all the exams and write all the assignments, as well as run a busy team, and hit all my work objectives. A new boat would be the prize for completing on time, or early. With every member of the group supporting each other, the four of us hell-bent on driving through the course managed to achieve the seemingly impossible. We were the only group which had zero dropouts, the only team where anyone finished early, the only team where over 60% finished on time. Sure, we had a couple of stragglers, but in the end, everyone made it. And lest you think that the aim was to do the course at the sake of learning, or contributing, nothing can be further from the truth. All of us learned and subsequently implemented, a great deal of very valuable things as a result of the course content. This was about accelerating our performance together.

Since Henley, I have set up several businesses and held senior roles at some global organisations, while continuing to create music, write, sail, and live life. What are the things I put this down to? The tools, tips, and suggestions I've picked up over the years through an avid interest in what it takes to be more productive. Have I reached terminal velocity? Absolutely not. I am still learning day by day how to accelerate my performance in certain areas, and how to slow down in others. It is a journey that has many stops and starts, twists and turns, ups and downs. But the best thing about adventures like that is that, as every car enthusiast will tell you, they provide the best opportunity to accelerate often, to practise how to reach your best performance.

Basic Philosophy of the Book

Pete was angry. He'd wanted a little support. He got the dismissive brush off.

He needed to succeed with this task as he'd had a few challenges with his boss in the past three or so months, so he'd spoken to Judy. She would know how to get this done. Judy was a high-flier in the team, always getting praise for doing an excellent job. Her tiara never seemed to slip. If anyone knew how to ace the task, it would be Judy.

Pete had spoken to her a few weeks back, and she'd agreed to help.

"I have a system", she smiled. "If you work it just like I do, then you too can get to the top of the class and get the evil witch off your back."

"Wow, thanks", he replied. "That easy?"

"Oh, yes. You have to follow it completely, though. I've spent years working it out."

It sounded like a great idea to learn from the best and put her system in place. That way, he could get the same kind of results, and he'd be laughing. According to her, if Pete wanted to do the best job possible, then he had to do 15 tasks, all in precisely the way that she prescribed. Every time he would veer away from her plan, she would chastise him, but the plan just didn't seem to be working for him.

The more he tried her way of working, the more he'd become frustrated, and so he asked her for some more guidance. That is when she brushed him off, telling him that he hadn't been doing as she'd said he should, and that as a result, the reason why it hadn't been working was because of him, and not her methods.

Pete was angry at himself for not being Judy for not working out what to do.

'Just another set of empty promises from a failsafe system that just didn't work!' he thought to himself.

This is not a 'Judy' type book or plan. I've spent too many years reading self-help books and have probably implemented only about 20% of what I've read, over a long period. The problem with so many of these books is that they make out it is easy. They tell a story about how the author's 10-point plan, followed to the letter will bring great rewards.

What so many of these books fail to recognise is that every single person is different.

Making lasting change is not easy. Accelerating requires considerable effort. Performing is exhausting and can be stressful.

The approach in this book is to present several core concepts with some practical tips designed to test, stretch and change you. There is no silver bullet. You will not wake up the day after you finish the book and be a different person. Lasting change is gradual. Habits need to be formed, and old habits broken. Accelerating your performance is possible, but it will take focus, discipline, concentration, and hard work. It is neither easy nor a quick fix. However, learning how to put some or all of the ideas contained in this book into practice will start you on your journey to changing, accelerating and the performance you desire.

I have sat through many motivational speeches from people who have achieved great things, and after them all, I feel a sense of energy and vigour. I feel I can achieve the goal. After all, they did, so I can. I will. But the big elephant in the room is the lack of connection with the hard work, the mental and physical toughness, the metal of the speech giver.

The amount of preparation Ellen MacArthur had to do to become the fastest single-handed, round the world sailor was extraordinary. Set aside her skills at navigation, meteorology, engineering, rigging, sail making, and maintenance. I am talking about the mental preparation, the physical conditioning, sponsorship, provisioning, filming and communications. Ellen did not achieve her goal because she set herself an aim to become the fastest sailor. She achieved her goal by each incremental step along the way, and the hours of mental, physical, and practical preparation. Then she had some luck for good measure.

Sir Steve Redgrave won Olympic gold in five consecutive games because he is a bloody-minded, hardworking, tower of a man at 6ft 5in and 16 stone. At school, my rowing coach was Peter Holmes, brother of Steve's first Olympic partner, Andy Holmes. Steve, Andy and two others won gold in 1984 in the coxed four. In 1988 he won two golds with Andy in the coxed and coxless pairs. Growing up with Steve Redgrave as a hero was inspiring. Training twice a day, six days a week was very hard. Knowing that Steve did that day in day out for over 20 years gave me a profound respect for his work ethic.

In 1997, he was diagnosed with type-2 diabetes, and yet with the right plan, and management of the illness, he was able to continue training right up to the Sydney Olympics in 2000 and win his 5th consecutive gold medal. If ever there was someone with mental toughness, physical endurance, an inspiring goal, and a solid plan to achieve it, it was Sir Steve.

So, accelerating your performance is certainly possible. Achieving your goals is almost certainly possible. But it requires effort and time. This is not a book for those with a 'get rich quick' mentality. This book will enable those who want to achieve something enough, to work on themselves, their environment, and their plans to get to where they want to be quicker than they would have done on their own.

Step by Step

"How am I going to achieve my target this year?" Joe felt a heavy, sinking feeling. He felt it every year at this time. "I get asked every year to project the business I can retain, grow, and get from new companies, and every year, they ignore what I've done." It was typical for management to dish out a higher number than the salesperson offered up for one excellent reason - sandbagging. Salespeople always have two numbers for every deal, the first is a high number, usually a lot higher than is probable, which they will use when asking for support from product, commercial, management, or any other department, and the second is lower than they think is reasonable to achieve, on the grounds that they can then over-achieve their target and earn-out some accelerators. Of course, Joe knew that Salesforce.com had significantly narrowed the opportunity to quote two different numbers, but he also knew it was pretty widespread amongst his colleagues.

Joe, however, had never played by those rules. He was as straight as they come, and had, in good faith, given what he considered to be the most likely outcome. He always had to accept an additional 10% each year, but this year it was 50%. "How the hell am I going to reach that?" he asked out loud.

When you have a large target, goal, or ambition, it is very easy to become paralysed by the enormity of it. Paralysis leads to inaction, and inaction leads to demotivation. So how do you guard against losing before you even get started?

Having a bold target is a good thing; being stretched as a salesperson is a good thing; pushing yourself is an excellent thing. At GE, Jack Welch, the CEO at the time, used to get all of the businesses to put forward their plans. These were the numbers that the accountants and markets were told were the targets. Every business was also allowed to dream - to come up with growth plans and numbers that could be reached if they weren't held back by things, or they had the resources they needed or other unconstrained dreams. These greater numbers were used internally to drive the business. Guess what happened year in and year out? The businesses achieved more than they had quoted the markets.

Why would that be the case? Because giving larger targets or goals pushes people to achieve more than they would have done if they'd set the lower number as the target. It may be that achievement is not quite at the dream level, but you can be sure it is usually significantly higher than the accountant's level. Having big dreams and goals is good as long as you know how to break down the tasks that get you there into manageable chunks.

Significant goals can be the biggest cause of inertia if you don't know how to break them down. You've heard a hundred times sayings such as 'by the yard, it's hard, by the inch it's a cinch'. All of us know that to drive from London to Edinburgh you have to drive one mile, followed by the next, and then the next, and eventually you will arrive. But when it comes to goals people set for themselves, it can be challenging to see a path.

Imagine that it's January the 6th and you want to get fit. The Christmas and New Year feeding frenzy is over, and you resolve to get fit. That is you and about a billion other people, too. What does 'getting fit' mean? It's not well enough specified, and there are no quantifiable goals to shoot for. It is a big ambition but with no process steps along the way.

You want to write a novel. You know that it needs to be somewhere in the region of 100,000 words. That is a lot of words. That seems like a massive task. How do you go about getting to the end? It is an enormous mountain in front of you. Somewhere in your mind, you know that it will require many hours of writing. You like the idea of having a book published, but you don't like the idea of writing it, just like you don't like the idea of running in the freezing January mornings to achieve your fitness goal.

Many people want their goals now, and if it seems like too much effort to get there or the mountain seems too high to climb, they make excuses and find ways of convincing themselves that it's not the right thing to do. "I'm not that unfit - especially compared to Dan", or "I don't have the time to write at the moment. I'll come back to it when the time's right."

If you want to achieve something, you need to set an Ultimate Goal, and then break the steps to getting there down into Stages. Nobody completes the Tour de France by looking at the finish line and dreaming. They finish it by taking each stage and making it count, et voila, at the end of all stages someone is crowned the winner. We will come back to Ultimate and Stage goals later in the book.

2. WHAT IS PERFORMANCE ACCELERATION?

Acceleration

When I ran European marketing for Tata Communications, I used to take customers to the experiential marketing track days of our sister company Jaguar Land Rover. At these events, we would get to drive around Thruxton, Gaydon, or Silverstone in various models of the latest Jaguar. By lap three or four, I'd feel a little more comfortable to open the taps fully as my instructor talked me around the track. Coming around the final bend with tonnes of lateral G-force was fun, lining the car up for an acceleration spurt out of the corner and over the line. Foot down. Power on. Pressure from the seat behind until the next braking zone when the feeling of deceleration was even more exaggerated. Endless adrenalin thrills as the car accelerated, braked, turned with G-force, and finally crossed the line for the last time in that session. I felt like a driving god.

The last session was in one of the new supercharged XJs with a professional racing driver taking the wheel. Boy was I glad to be the front seat passenger, and not the poor sod consigned to car sickness hell in the back. The traction control was off, he put his foot to the floor, slid around corners, and showed me what acceleration was really like. I had been a rank amateur.

Before diving into the things you can to do to accelerate, let's look at acceleration itself. For those that found physics either boring or easy, I apologise. This is pretty simple stuff, on the GCSE curriculum for 14-16-year olds, but for those of us who forgot most of what we learned at school the day the last exams were over, it's a useful refresher.

Acceleration is measured in metres per second squared. Or put another way, it is the change in velocity/speed (metres per second) divided by the time taken (seconds). If you know the speed at the start, and the end, and the time taken, you can work out the acceleration. So, a car that starts travelling at 25 m/s, and over 5 seconds reaches 35 m/s has accelerated at 2 m/s2.

That is the theory over with, but the fundamentals are that the speed increases over time.

In the pursuit of accelerating your own personal performance, you must remember that this is a gradual process that takes time. You need patience. You need to focus on incremental speed changes. If you try to accelerate too fast, you may end up frustrated. If you accelerate hard without changing gears at the right time, you'll redline, with the engine screaming, acceleration halting, and achievement ending.

Strong Foundation

For any vehicle to accelerate, it needs to be constructed out of the appropriate material. A car with a chassis made from the lead in your pencil is not going to accelerate very fast or far. It will break in two. That's why no car chassis are made of pencils. Pencil lead is made of carbon or graphite. Drop a pencil, and the lead will break.

You might conclude that carbon is not a great material for making things that need to be strong. But diamonds are also made of carbon, and they are so strong that they are used to cut through the toughest substances known to man.

Take some microscopic carbon filaments though, bond enough of them together in a carbon fibre polymer, and you end up with a material that is both very light, and extremely strong. Consequently, the chassis, most of the suspension, and the bodywork of a formula one car are made from carbon fibre.

The chassis needs to be strong enough to cope with any kind of movement, but to be able to handle reasonable acceleration, it needs to be very strong. The forces that are put through a car when it accelerates quickly are significant. To accelerate from 0-60 in 2.5 seconds means a force of over 7,000 newtons being applied. In technical terms, that's 'a lot'.

For you to be able to accelerate your performance and reach your goal, you need to think about your own 'chassis'. What are you made from, physically, mentally, and emotionally? Is the composition of all parts robust enough?

Engine with Grunt

The engine of a Bugatti Veyron Super Sport has an 8.0-litre engine and puts out a staggering 1,084 bhp. It can get from 0-100 kmh (62 mph) in 2.46 seconds. A 2013 F1 car only had a 2.4-litre engine but put out a miserly 750 bhp. It gets from 0-62 mph in around 2 seconds, so is no slouch. These two cars are impressive, but they are totally different. One is heavy and needs all-wheel drive.

The other is very light, has no roof, and only powers the rear wheels. One thing they do have in common is that they both have engines that have serious grunt.

The cheetah is the world's fastest land mammal and can accelerate from 0-60mph in around 3 seconds. Their hind legs are exceptionally powerful with large muscles designed for sprinting. A flexible spine, claws, and light characteristics make it perfect for sprinting to catch its prey. But while it would put most cars to shame in a short drag race, it cannot sustain the speed over great distances. Its 'engine' is built for short sharp bursts that give it the speed it needs to hunt.

So many things factor in the ability to accelerate, over and above the engine size, but you can be sure that without an engine with enough grunt you won't be able to accelerate, even if you fix all of the other things.

An engine takes in fuel, ignites it, and burns in an explosion to push pistons and turn that energy into heat and movement. You need to have an engine with enough power to accelerate with, and unlike a cheetah, yours will need to be able to accelerate for a long time, as you get ever closer to your goal. What is the fuel you have? What will ignite your passion every day? How much fuel do you have? What bhp do you put out daily?

Tyres for Traction

The best demonstration of different types of tyre is in formula one. In the dry, the teams can choose from two pre-prescribed types, usually a prime, harder slick, and an option (or softer) slick. The rubber compound has been specially formulated to grip in a certain way and to degrade over time. By the middle of a race, there are marbles of rubber all over the track, parallel to the racing line.

If the race is wet, then the teams can choose from intermediates or full wet tyres. If it's a bit wet, the intermediates will suffice with their minimal treads, but if it is seriously Malaysia or Brazil type wet, then the bigger grooved treads on the full wets will clear the water, enabling the car to grip the track. Get the choice of tyre wrong, and the driver will be in all sorts of trouble. Run the full wets when the track is drying out, and the rubber won't take it, will degrade, making the car run way too slowly. Run the intermediates with too much water, and the car will aquaplane off at the first bend.

One thing is for sure, without rubber on your tyres, your finely tuned engine bolted into the strongest and lightest of chassis, is unlikely to get you accelerating very fast. In BBC2s 'Top Gear' programme, Clarkson, May and Hammond renovated a Jaguar XJS convertible to run on train tracks. In place of tyres, they added train wheels. The problem was evident as Clarkson gunned the engine, and screeching sparks flew as the metal on metal produced virtually no traction at all. As usual with their capers, they found a solution, but this point shows that it is down to the grip you have underneath you as to how quickly, or far you'll be able to accelerate.

There is a saying which goes 'That's where the rubber hits the road', meaning 'That's what matters'. All the rest is academic unless the rubber is firmly placed on the road. A great engine with loads of grunt but no rubber on the road will make the wheels spin, wasting lots of energy. If you are not actually travelling anywhere, then your chassis doesn't need to be that strong.

The road is your terrain, and the tyres are the things that give you grip and traction. If you like, the tyres are how you engage with your terrain. Engage with the wrong type of compound, and you won't accelerate as much as you could. If the going is wet, get the choice of engagement wrong, and you may find yourself surfing off in the other direction at the first obstacle around which to navigate.

Tyres, in our analogy, are your attitude - your EQ, your approach with colleagues, clients, projects, and obstacles. Get this right, and you stand a much better chance of making it to where you want to get to and accelerate faster than you were able to do before.

Changing Gear

Every gear in a car has an acceleration curve. If you are in second gear and you accelerate, you will pick up speed quite rapidly at first, then it will continue to increase, but then it will reach a point at which it very quickly tapers off. If you carry on in second gear, the engine revs will still climb, but your acceleration rate will decline. This is when you need to change gear to third, wherein, you can accelerate more, and as your speed progresses, your engine revs climb, and your acceleration tapers off again.

Knowing how to change gears is a skill that all manual car drivers learn. Smoothly, with no gear grating, and speedily, while raising the right foot off the accelerator. We take it for granted when driving that this is a pretty basic skill, but if you want to get the maximum acceleration, you need to master the skill, just as much as judging the right timing for making a shift.

The judgement comes down to several things - what the engine sounds like, what you are used to doing, whether you are attempting to overtake a slow-moving lorry on a slightly tight bend of a relatively busy road, or you want to beat that Porsche off the lights. Everyone has a usual driving style. It's what you feel comfortable doing for the majority of your journeys. I tend to drive like I'm in a hurry to get to the other end. Am I always in a hurry? Pretty much when I'm on my own. When I'm with other people or trying to achieve something specific, however, then the right speed and right acceleration depend on many different factors.

There is little point in racing to the finish line on your own if those around you can't keep up. Sometimes the right thing to do is change gear down a level or two to match the level at which others feel comfortable. Once they are at the gentler speed you set, you can increase the pace a little, gradually, over time, and they will most likely follow. Get to the point at which a gear change is needed, and you can all change up together.

Imagine a situation where you need a group of people to work together to complete a task. You are leading the team in the development of a marketing campaign, which will enable your customers to take advantage of a discounted, limited time offer on one of your product packages. You have loads of ideas in your head, and you can easily see what the campaign could look like. You have done this kind of thing many times before, and so can cut straight to the crucial tasks that need to be done. On your team, though, you have a couple of less experienced people, and one old-timer, who is set in their ways. Your job indeed is to get the task done, but it is also to lead the team to get it done. So, you have to change down a gear, getting to their speed, and gradually applying pressure to the pedal as you bring them all up to speed. Before you know it, you are changing gears and finishing together.

It is a real skill to be able to pace and lead. Not just teams, but yourself too. Some days you won't feel like doing what needs to be done. Some of those days will be down to indiscipline, some because you are exhausted, and others due to ill health. You must recognise which of these is the reason and then set about pacing yourself. If that means going slower for a time, then so be it. You know that you can gather momentum, and speed up, eventually leading yourself out of the temporary slump, towards completion of your goals.

In a following chapter, we'll look at the foundation to your potential and success - YOU. Having a good understanding of yourself is the first step to realising your ambitions. Knowing how to manage yourself effectively is the first step towards accelerating your performance.

Performance

Perform -Verb - to carry out, accomplish or fulfil and action, task or function. To work, function or do something to a specified standard.

Performance - Noun - an act of staging or presenting a play, concert, or another form of entertainment. A person's rendering of a dramatic role, song, or piece of music.

The synonyms for performance include execution, fulfilment, and accomplishment.

Performance, in the business context, is about attaining a goal. Without a goal, you have no idea how you are performing.

Have you ever been in a stage production, a musical concert, or sporting activity? Perhaps you have to search your memory for half-remembered episodes from school that you'd rather forget. Or maybe you have fond memories of playing for the netball B team, or J16 rowing crew, the Christmas carol concert in the choir, or the second violin part you played in the Dvorak New World Symphony. Maybe you are still a pillar of the AMDRAM society, sing in the church choir, or play Cricket for Hartley Wintney's first team on a Sunday. I'm sure that lurking there is a memory of a time when you were ready for the performance. Either the house lights went down low, or the whistle went for the start of the match. Whatever the case, at that moment, everything else would have emptied from your mind, as you focused on your task at hand. As the conductor waved his arms, and you counted your two-bar rest before the tricky little semiquaver passage, or the cox calmly ordered you all to burn for 20 strokes in order to steal a canvas on the other crew, you were incapable of thinking about anything else other than performing your task to the best of your ability. For the 1st 11, the brass quintet, the cast of the school play. For yourself. And, when you finished, you knew you had done something extraordinary. Sure, you may not have won, or played like the City of Birmingham Symphony Orchestra, or acted like a thespian from the RSC, but you had performed to the very best you could.

You had a goal. To win. To play or sing an excellent performance of Brahms' Requiem. To move people in the audience with the story you were telling on stage.

You executed. You accomplished. You fulfilled. Your performance mattered.

Performing is one of those things that you can learn. It is about a goal, a focus, a direction, a plan, a team, and achieving.

Remember the performance of which you are proudest. Was it easy to perform at that level? Did you have to practise and work hard to get there?

I remember skippering a boat in a spring series regatta on the Solent. As a crew, we had raced together for a few years. That weekend, over the four races we battled the wind, a nasty Solent chop, and 20 other boats. The boats were identical in every way, apart from the crew.

One design racing is about the crew, and how well they perform as a team. Each member of the crew has their job, from the helmsman to the foredeck, navigator, trimmers and the pitman. Four races, of which the worst result would be discarded, meant we needed to score in position 1 or 2 in each race to stand a chance of taking the trophy. That was going to require an individual performance from every member of the crew, and a collective performance we would all be proud of. We did well in race one but had a shocker in race two. The pressure was on to make sure we came 1st or 2nd in each of the last two. All of the years of racing together, all the spinnaker hoists and drops we had drilled, the tacks, gybes, tactical wind shift spotting, and local tidal stream knowledge paid off as we clinched the regatta win by just 1 point. Everyone was very proud. All were exhausted. Not one of us had spent a second thinking about work, rugby, motor racing, or filing our tax returns while we'd been performing.

In summary, performance requires an unwavering focus on the goal and the tasks needing to be performed in order to reach the goal. It also involves a lot of hard work. No-one steps onto a boat on a grey March weekend in the

Solent, never having sailed before and wins. In fact, we only won two regattas in over ten years of racing, so even if you work hard, you still may not achieve the ultimate goal.

Performance requires many other vital factors.

Great Driver

In Formula 1, teams spend millions on securing the best possible drivers. They are looking for fit, short, light drivers with lightning-quick reactions, who are hungry to win. They are also expected to manage their races so that they don't crash (too often), get their fuel use and tyre wear right, and intelligently do everything at just the right time to make the overtake manoeuvres stick. They need to be experts in different weather conditions, at different circuits, with their unique twists, turns, bumps, and curbs. And they must be able to cope with constant travel, living away from home for much of the year.

Then, once they are out of the car, they are expected to engage with the media relentlessly, answering the same questions over and over again, while smiling and making it sound like it's the first time they have been asked. If all that were not a lot already, they need to bring sponsorship money to the team too.

Most of the things above can be learned. What is not learned is the innate talent. They were born with it. Lightning-quick reactions, the ability to take risks, get that little bit extra out of a car than the average person.

They were often born to parents, usually their dad, who was more obsessed with motorsport than they were at eight years old. A life dedicated to karting, followed by one of rising through the lower formulas, before eventually hitting the big time. Their innate talent is hardcoded in their DNA. Their opportunity to make use of it, refine their skills, amass the experience, and become a winner is created by nurture and opportunity.

The analogy extends into our own lives as we reach for the best performance possible. Imagine you want to run the London Marathon in under 4 hours. You will need to be able to run, then gradually get your split times per mile down to the right level, gradually increase your strength and distance. You will have to raise sponsorship money. You will be asked the same questions by lots of friends and family, where you will need to answer them as if it is the first time you've been asked. Your diet will need to be modified to make sure you are getting enough of the right types of nutrient at the right part of your training cycle. You may not be able to finish with the front runners, but you will want to focus on your personal best and hitting your target.

How can you turn yourself into a great runner? What are the characteristics needed?

Persistence, lots of practice and the ability to run.

Strong Team

How many people can you name who have become really successful entirely on their own? Go on, name just one.

There are small successes all of us have every day of our lives that are entirely ours. If your goal is to bake a cake and you make a fabulous chocolate one on your own, you have been successful. If you decide to teach yourself the guitar and can then play Hotel California after just a few sessions, you have been successful on your own. But if you want to perform at the highest level, you cannot do it alone. The person who wins MasterChef has a team of people helping them along the way, from the friends and family they test their recipes out on, to the butcher and greengrocer who help them choose the best possible ingredients, to the chefs that inspire them. To get a distinction in your grade 8 guitar exam will mean needing support and guidance from a teacher, access to an audience to perform in front of, and a few John Williams recordings to inspire you to greatness.

On the surface, you might look at yourself and think 'It was I who achieved my goal' but dig deeper and you'll soon see that your wife, husband, or partner played a part. At work, your colleagues, your mentor, and maybe your boss will have contributed.

During the BT Global Challenge yacht race in 1996/7, Mike Golding proved that a strong team could dominate. Out of the six legs, covering 30,000 miles the wrong way around the world, competing against 13 other amateur crews, Golding's boat 'Group 4' won five. They came second in the other leg. Overall, they won by two days and almost six hours over their nearest rival, and 15 days, 13 hours over the last-place finisher. The lessons learned on leadership and teamwork were captured in a book called 'Global Challenge - Leadership lessons from The World's Toughest Yacht Race'. The crews were made from ordinary people who volunteered to spend nine months competing in this gruelling event. They were all amateurs and even paid to take part. The skippers were professional, sea-hardened sailors, with multiple circumnavigations each under their belts.

While many of the other skippers coached their crews to perform several different roles on the boat, to give everyone a chance to perform multiple tasks throughout the race, Mike Golding opted for a one person, one job approach. Initially, this was a cause for concern. All the members of the crew had paid a lot of money to participate, and no-one wanted to be just a galley slave for nine months. But Mike led the team - that was his job. If he was to win the race, he needed a strong team around him.

By the time the race began on 29th September, every member of the Group 4 crew knew their jobs inside and out. They knew that their own role was as important as any other job on the boat. They had a purpose. They were drilled. They were ready. And they won - handsomely.

Mike Golding had said to his crew that the day he could stay below decks all day with nothing to do was the day he had turned them into a fully performing team. The strength of the team made the difference.

Now, cast your mind back to the world of F1. The drivers might be the glory boys - the dashing young men driving on a knife-edge, commanding the multi-million salaries, but the pit crew can win or lose a race for the team. The engineers can make the right choices with the aerodynamics, and other smart things, or the wrong ones. The strategists can pit a driver so they can return to the track in clean air or ruin a race by forcing him back into a group of back-markers. The entire team needs to be firing on all cylinders for the raw talent of the glory hunters to create legends.

You can have success on your own, but to accelerate your performance, you need a highly focused team around you.

Best Preparation

"The time to repair the roof is when the sun is shining" - John F Kennedy.

Very sound words. It makes little sense to attempt to replace a few roof tiles during a storm. The only problem is that while the sun is shining, there are so many other more pleasant things to be doing; enjoying the great out-doors, barbecuing with friends, reading a book, or even gardening. The last thing any of us wants to do (certainly in the UK) is to waste one of the nine days of sun-filled summer we usually get each year, mending the roof.

There are a few examples of preparation which show its importance. When Ellen Macarthur sailed solo around the world in her yacht Kingfisher during the Vendee Globe, she slept for only a few hours a day. In fact, this is normal for every round the world yachtsman or woman. Ellen was responsible for everything on her boat, from the navigation and the sail setting to the seaworthiness of the boat. Years of training prepared her for the actual sailing. A solo circumnavigation of the UK as little more than a child on a Corribee 21, and plenty of ocean miles under her belt to qualify to enter the race. Years of hard graft until there wasn't much that she didn't know about how to sail a boat well. How to sail a boat fast. But for a boat to take a pounding for around three months, without any outside assistance, she would need to keep a vigilant watch on every line, cleat, sail, piece of machinery, spar, bolt, wave and squall. She had to anticipate what might be a point of weakness and either replace or repair it before it got to the point of failure. Every minute of her waking hours, she would busy herself with repairing and preparing.

Weather is temperamental. In the ocean, it can be fickle, and lack of preparation can cause a severe problem. An otherwise cloudless sky with light to no breeze can turn within an instant to a fierce squall which would almost certainly rip the lightweight sails and overpower the boat dangerously. Ellen would continuously watch for patches of cloud, which would signify that the wind will get up, even if only for a brief period. And as she was racing, she needed every extra puff of wind channelled to make the boat sail faster. In anticipation, she would affect a sail change, replacing the light wind headsails for a smaller, more robust one. Perhaps even reduce the sail area of the mainsail too.

The wind filled in, the boat was pressed hard, the speed increased. No damage was done. And again, the wind subsided, requiring another sail change to capture the little breeze that remained to help power her along.

How many of us would have done that upwards of 20 times a day, with only a handful of hours sleep to allow us to recover from the physically strenuous activity?

Then in the Southern Ocean, the most tempestuous of places to sail, with the threat of waves big enough to swamp the yacht, and icebergs below a certain latitude, Ellen had to scale the mast to make a repair. On her own, with the boat powering under sail through the waves, trusting in the autopilot and good fortune, she scaled the mast and did what she knew needed to be done. That was preparation for the continuing days of an onslaught that mother nature would throw her way. While up the mast she was buffeted around like a rag doll on a stick, finding her leg often slipping between the sail and the mast, knowing that one freak wave could throw the boat into an uncontrollable broach, trapping and most probably snapping her leg in two.

Ellen was prepared with knowledge about how to do her job - how to sail, navigate, go fast, repair things. She was prepared physically - sleep deprivation training, strength. She was prepared mentally - she knew that she would face danger and hardship, but she never let those break her. She had learned to be mentally tough.

'Taking on the World' is Ellen's story, filmed while she was racing to become the youngest ever person to complete the Vendee Globe. She finished the race in second place but was crowned as the fastest woman ever to sail around the world solo (Feb 11th, 2001). It is a documentary that is worth watching to understand how preparing technically, physically and mentally can make all the difference. And if the accolade of being the fastest female solo circumnavigator wasn't enough for her, she used the Vendee experience as preparation for becoming the fastest person on the planet to complete a solo round the world journey. On Monday 7th February 2005, Ellen took the record, completing the solo voyage in 71 days, 14 hours, 18 minutes and 6 seconds.

Focus

For many years I worked at a company called Equant, which, after about two years of being there, was bought by France Telecom. Before it rebranded to Orange, Equant was a distinctly global telecoms operator. It was just about the only one that had a genuinely global offering, being able to provide services to companies in 220 countries and territories. The thing that made Equant different from the likes of BT, AT&T, Telefonica, Singtel, Telstra or T-Systems was that it did not have a 'home market'. Equant hadn't grown from being a local telecoms company in the UK to be international (BT), or Australia (Telstra) or the

US (AT&T). It grew out of the airline industry's need to connect every airport in every country. That is why the network coverage was more global in nature than any other operator on the planet. While other telecoms service providers could connect well in their home territories, they had to service customers with some partial international capability cobbled together with services from other operators. Equant, however, focused 100% on the global needs of companies.

The focus was clear to customers and employees alike. The offering was simple - if a company needed a global network connecting multiple locations in many different countries, then Equant was the only really logical choice. Even better still, if the customer needed to get to the hard to reach places, like certain parts of Africa. For a time, Equant grew at a phenomenal rate.

Focus is all about what you are doing at the present moment - keeping your actions trained on the centre of the picture, the area that is in focus, is bright and has colour. It is not good enough to know what you want to achieve (your goal). We can all state a goal and then succumb to distraction, losing focus on what we need to do to achieve it. Every new year, millions of people give themselves new goals, and every year, most of those people fail to achieve them. Why? Because other things get in the way. Life happens. Other things become a higher priority, so the goals wither and die. These distractions cause all of us to lose focus, and there isn't one amongst us who doesn't get distracted by a hundred things a day. Just start with Facebook, Twitter, EastEnders, Corrie, that glass of wine, or the gossip by the coffee machine.

Keeping a laser focus can make the difference between performing and performing really well. Get it right, and you can accelerate your performance much more quickly.

Take Sir Steve Redgrave, one of the world's most successful Olympians of all time. I've mentioned him before, as the bloody-minded inspiration who spurred me on to row competitively at school. While I only ever achieved a silver medal at the national championships, he won Gold at five consecutive Olympic games. At the World Championships in 1999, Redgrave was rowing with Cracknell, Pinsent and Coode in the coxless four. In the final, with about 500 metres of the race remaining, it was clear they had a chance to win by a considerable margin and clinch the world record. They had an opportunity to dominate their rivals and show them who was boss. Show them emphatically that they'd have to settle for silver in Sydney a year later. James Cracknell called for them to 'Go!'. Steve shouted 'No!'. James shouted for them to 'Go!' again. Once more, Steve bellowed 'No!'. As the giant in age, experience and stature of the boat, Steve's say weighed more, and so they missed the world record, and only just won the race by a second.

Needless to say, the rest of the crew was perplexed, and a few words were exchanged. James asked, 'What was that about?'. Steve replied, 'Would you rather the opposition go away and train all winter before Sydney, thinking they need to improve by five seconds or one second?'

They won Gold (with Foster replacing Coode) at Sydney, but I bet you don't remember the winning margin. History records the win, and our memories don't retain the details. Well, they won by just 0.7 seconds. Had their opposition trained to be another five seconds faster, Redgrave would only be a four-time Olympian.

With age and experience, Sir Steve Redgrave was able to blot out the distraction of the possible record and the thrill of smashing a win at that particular race, in favour of the real goal. That is a masterclass in knowing your real goal and maintaining your focus completely. That is why he will be remembered as one of the greatest Olympians of all time.

Mental Toughness

To succeed, to achieve something remarkable, you need to be tough. Mentally tough. So, what do I mean by that?

Tony Bullimore was a yachtsman. He entered the 1996 Vendee Globe single-handed yacht race aboard his boat Exide Challenger. The Vendee requires an incredible amount of preparation as we saw with the story of Dame Ellen Macarthur.

On January the 5th 1997, Exide Challenger capsized in the Southern Ocean. It was a fair assumption that it would have been lost to the vast, freezing and hostile conditions. How could anyone survive with an upturned boat for company, in one of the most inhospitable places on earth? Not only is the Southern Ocean ferocious, but it is about as far from any other civilisation as you can get – the astronauts on the International Space Station were closer to his stricken vessel than any human on the planet! A rescue attempt would take days at best, and at worst never locate him.

Another competitor, Thierry Dubois, had also capsized and so the Royal Australian Navy launched a rescue mission. First, they found and rescued Thierry. Then they sailed further south to where an Orion aircraft had spotted Tony's upturned hull. After six days, the HMAS Adelaide's RIB was launched and motored to the floating wreck. Almost nobody could have imagined there would be a reply to the taps they made on the outside of the hull. But miracles can happen, and on hearing the tapping, Tony swam out from the air pocket he'd been living in for almost a week. He was rescued and taken back to the Frigate. He and Thierry were later returned safe and sound to Perth to be reunited with their loved ones.

What is remarkable about this story is that Tony Bullimore survived in an air pocket inside an upturned hull. There would have been no light; he would have been very, very cold. He had no food other than a chocolate bar. He had water all around him, but none that he could drink. I know that I would have struggled to keep going under these circumstances. I'm sure I am not alone in this. How many of us would have been lying in the upturned hull in the dark, with no food, cold and wet and thought to ourselves 'I'm in the Southern Ocean. Everyone will assume I've drowned' No one is coming to find me'? Maybe we could have coped with a day or two, as adrenaline and a deep-seated survival instinct can help keep us going for a short time. But after three days. Four. Five?

By all accounts, he should have died. Physically, he should have succumbed to hypothermia or dehydration. But he is one of the toughest men out there - mentally. He refused to give up. It was not an option for him to die. He clung to hope. He made it work until somebody knocked at the door.

And not only did he survive, but he had the mental toughness to continue yacht racing when in 2005 he skippered a boat that came second in the Oryx Quest.

This is rather an extreme story, but as an example, it forces us to ask whether we have what it takes - up top. Do we have the mental toughness to carry through with our goals? Would we be able to carry on if faced with large, and seemingly insurmountable problems?

To achieve goals and accelerate your performance, you will need a certain amount of mental toughness. There are other words I can think of, too, such as willpower, bloody-mindedness and discipline. The ability to know the goal and focus on the tasks at hand in spite of other things, be they external or internal, getting in your way.

How often have you set yourself a goal or a task and not completed it? Is it ten times a year? Ten times a month? Ten times a day?

Take weight loss, for example. Losing weight requires you to take in fewer calories than you burn in a day. Not just for one day. Not even for a few days. But every day until you reach your desired weight. But how many people have the willpower or mental toughness to carry through with that?

The reason many people fail is that they allow excuses to be OK. They give themselves rewards for 'having worked hard today', for 'having lost a few pounds', or because they just like cheese too much not to have that extra slice. And who can resist the allure of a takeaway when you've been slaving away all week and want to have a night off?

But all of these are just excuses. If you set a goal, and you really want to achieve that goal, then you must take accountability for it, and being accountable means not allowing excuses to become a reason for not achieving it.

Nobody needs another slice of cheese. No-one needs to order a takeaway. A glass or three of wine is not necessary. They are all lovely. They are all fabulous. And you can eat and drink them all. But not when your goal is set. Not when you have some bigger cause to aim for.

Being mentally tough is to see things in black or white. Either you are intent on losing weight, or you are not. Either you are writing a book, or you aren't. Either you are training for a marathon, or you aren't. If you are deciding to do any of those things, then commit to them and do them 100%. That requires mental toughness.

Tony Bullimore's choice was black or white. Do everything possible to ensure survival for as long as possible or to die.

Mental toughness is a skill that can be learned and combined with goal setting, focus and excellent preparation can make all the difference to accelerating your personal performance.

Goal

It's easy to think of the word goal in the context of football or other sports, as a place where you put a ball to score. However, it stems from middle English around the 1530s and signified the endpoint of a race. The first use of it figuratively, meaning 'the object of an effort' came only ten years later in 1540. I much prefer the figurative meaning since the sporting references have connotations of winning or beating others. A goal that is the 'object of an effort' can be large or small, significant or insignificant, for its own sake or to achieve something. You can collect many goals together, all of different types, to form a much more critical, ultimate goal.

Let's say I have a goal to make a living from writing. Making a living from writing is the ultimate goal, but without amassing quite a number of sub-goals, or as I call them 'stage goals' I won't stand a chance of making a living at it. The ultimate goal does not indicate how to achieve it. It is specific and measurable. It may or may not be attainable. It is relevant, purely on the basis that it is my desired goal. But as yet it isn't time-bound. I could set a deadline, but if I did, I would still be none the wiser as to how I'd achieve it. What's missing is the bit about **how** to attain it.

Attainment covers many things, including ability in the form of skills, knowledge and resources now, potential to acquire more skills, knowledge and resources in the future, and knowing the steps needed to make the ultimate goal a reality. Assuming you have good skills, knowledge and resources now and can add to these, over time, the part that's left is the step-by-step journey to reach your goal - 'stage goals'.

In the Tour de France, they have stages, each one a gruelling race in its own right. In Formula 1 there are 20 or so races in a season, each one fiercely contested. In the Olympic sailing events, each race provides points, the total of which determines who wins the Gold medal. For Sir Bradley Wiggins or Chris Froome to win the Tour de France meant having to do well enough in each of the stages to build enough of a lead to make certain of the result.

Every goal can be split down into sub-goals in ever decreasing increments. To make a living at writing, I must write books. To write books, I must write chapters. To write chapters, I must write a certain number of words. To sell books, I must market them. To market them, I need to know who is likely to buy them. To find this out, I must conduct research. To appeal to buyers, I must understand what they want to read. To enable people to buy the books, I must distribute them as physical books and as e-books. To publish them, I must discover how to do that. And before I can even start writing, I must have a good idea, structure it and make it flow logically so that the reader benefits from it.

I can set goals for every part of the writing, publishing, marketing, and selling processes. More than 'I can', **I must**, for without setting stage goals along the way for every part of the process, there is no way I will ever achieve my ultimate goal.

Stage goals cannot be underestimated. Without them, you cannot know how far along the journey you have come and still have to travel. You have nothing to track. You won't know where you're going, or how to get there. Stage goals keep you honest - they provide a framework for accountability so that you cannot simply shrug and offer up excuses.

Stage goals enable you to beat procrastination too. Studies have shown that people who start a small, even tiny task towards a goal become motivated by the actions they have taken. Remember my friend Martin's wise words? "Doing doesn't come from motivation. Motivation comes from doing." Intuitively he knew that to be the case. The science of Psychology has proven him to be right.

Breaking down tasks into smaller bite-sized chunks means that every one of them is manageable and perhaps even easy. As time progresses and more of these small tasks are completed, you can suddenly find that you've achieved an enormous amount.

We'll look into goal setting in detail in part 2. Until then, ask yourself this question: "To achieve my ultimate goal, what stage goals could I commit to that would start me on my journey?" Write them down, and we'll revisit them later.

Must know when to stop

Accelerating is good if you have all the right elements lined up in the right direction. If you know your goal, you can set a direction and mark waypoints along your route as stage goals. You have the right foundation, the energy to proceed; you're sure you can get good traction off the line. You've been practising gear changes for a while, so they should be fine too. As you prepare to set off, you feel comfortable that the team around you is great. You are focused, feeling mentally strong. You've never been more prepared. All is good for the start.

Three. Two. One. Go. You're pressed back into your seat as you accelerate forwards. The speed is climbing rapidly. Adrenalin is pumping. You're achieving each of the stage goals. Before you know it, you're closer to your goal. This is suddenly fun.

When I set a goal and concentrate fully, everything else seems to vanish into the background. I have been both praised and criticised for being very, or too focused in the past. My world can get consumed by my goals, of which I have many, and this means that I achieve things. Unfortunately, two other side effects happen as well.

First, I know I tend to become mildly obsessed with achieving my goals and exclude everything else from my life while I go for it. This is not very healthy, either for me or those around me. Sure, it's true that to accelerate we all need to focus, and that means minimising the distractions. But don't make the mistake of thinking that your friends, family and important tasks are distractions. You need to do well at your job, so you keep a roof over your head, and that requires focus. There are plenty of other mundane tasks, like paying the bills or shopping that must also get done. Your friends and family are an essential part of your team, even if they are not directly involved in the current goal you're trying to achieve. They are your support mechanism, providing love and friendship as you go for whatever it is you want to get done.

This book is about helping you to accelerate your performance, and the tips and tools in part 2 will give you a solid basis for being able to do just that. What this book is not is advocating that the achievement of a goal, no matter how big or small, is more important than the things that really matter in life - safety, (good) relationships, health and the ability to give an receive love.

The second side effect I can suffer from is burn-out. It has taken me years to get over this, and it's not hard to lapse back into it. Burn out comes from doing something too much and is a sign of a lack of balance. As human beings, we need a variety of work, play, sleep, fun, concentration, food, love, enjoyment and purpose. If we don't get these in balance, then we suffer the consequences. My mind used to race, thinking about all the things that needed to be done, what all the tasks would be to reach the stage goals. The way I shut my brain down was to commit these to paper, so I didn't have to hold everything in my mind. I used to drive myself to put more hours or effort into writing, web design, fitness, or weight loss to the point where I either became too fatigued mentally or physically to carry on. Too much of anything leads to boredom, no matter how interesting the subject, or enjoyable it is. Anyone who doesn't believe that should ask a couple who has been trying to have a baby for months whether the act of making babies is still fun anymore. They will both groan (and not in a good way either!).

It's about the balance of activity or task with the many areas of your own life. While working as a freelance copywriter, I would spend a couple of hours writing (using the Pomodoro technique - more on this later) and then go and watch an episode of 'Breaking Bad' or play the piano and try to write a song. Then I'd come back to writing for a couple of hours more. This worked for me as it helped my brain switch gears entirely and the result was better writing in less time than if I'd just tried to slog through.

You must learn when to stop. When to rest. When to change down a gear. How to listen to yourself and those around you.

You will only be able to go as fast as the weakest element will allow, and sometimes that will be you.

As Fast as the Weakest Element

On 20th September 2006, Top Gear presenter Richard Hammond crashed at a speed of 288.3 mph (464 km/h). Although this was not an official attempt at the land speed record on one of the runs the telemetry suggested he reached 314.4 mph (506 km/h), which would have been a British record. I managed 130 mph in a Vauxhall Vectra once, and that felt quite fast enough for me.

Richard had spent the day without incident at an airfield in York, filming for a feature on the programme to be aired later that year. Then, on the last run of the day, to get a couple of extra scenes, he got the jet-powered Vampire car fired up and climbing towards 300 mph. Suddenly the right front tyre failed, and despite one of the parachutes deploying to reduce his speed, the car veered on to the grass and spun over. By the time the car landed on its roll cage, it was still travelling at 232 mph (373.4 km/h). Richard Hammond's crash helmet was dragged along the ground (upside down) as the roll cage dug into the grass and finally came to a stop. Had the diminutive presenter been any taller it's conceivable that he'd have been decapitated.

He suffered significant injuries, and to this day still suffers from emotional problems and memory loss. If there is one upside, it's that while he was in the hospital, he forgot he was married and tried to chat his wife up. What a fantastic gift to be able to look at your wife with fresh eyes and after many years and find her just as wonderful.

No matter how prepared you are, it only takes one weak element to ruin your day. In this instance, Richard Hammond's training kicked in instinctively. He immediately braked the car, steered into the blowout and deployed the parachute, thereby killing the engine and jet afterburner. The verdict after the crash was that he responded like a pro and it is unlikely anyone else could have handled it better. He knew how to stop, and when a life-threatening weakness threatened him, he managed to stop.

As you accelerate towards your ultimate goal, keep an eye on all parts of your vehicle, team and self. When the weakest one gives out, it's time to slow down, mend or replace it, do a safety check and then get going again.

Know Your Safe Speed

I used to ride a motorcycle. I passed my test many years ago but gave it up in favour of safer and drier transport. Then at the age of 41, I decided to get another one. Life would be no fun at all if you couldn't indulge in a mid-life crisis or two, would it?

When I took my test, and for the years I rode around as a student, I had a 125cc Honda. I even worked as a courier during one hot summer in London. Utter madness! Eleven hours in the saddle in a city that's way too full of traffic and pollution was like playing a daily game of Russian Roulette. And when I'd return home at the end of the day the part of my face not covered by the helmet was black with soot. Still, it paid some bills and kept my adrenals working well.

After a gap of almost 14 years, I opted for a 600cc Honda. Not your 'instant death' Fireblade, but a mid-sized engine. All I wanted to do was enjoy being outside and potter around my local area, with the odd longer journey into London.

"We'd advise you to take a refresher course", the nice gentleman said as we completed the paperwork. "It's quite a bit bigger than you were used to riding and it's been a while."

Of course, he was absolutely right. But I had other ideas. Never short of confidence in my own driving ability, I wondered how hard it could be to control an engine more than four times the size of the last one I rode. And anyway, everyone always tells you that you never forget how to ride a bike, so that's exactly what I did. Throttle screaming, jerky and completely unbalanced, I rode away from the shop on the high street and made it the mile back home. Just! I needed some practice.

Over the following days and weeks, I spent time with my bike, feeling like I was breaking it in. Taming it. In reality, I was just learning how to ride again. It took a few months before I felt confident enough to take it out on a motorway, and when I did, it was horrendous! On a 125cc the fastest road I could go on was an A road with a 60-mph speed limit, though that applied to all other vehicles except for mine, which would get up to about 50mph if I was lucky (it was old). On my new bike, I could accelerate past 80mph in the blink of an eye, and it was terrifying. Being a tall rider and the bike being more of a 'sit up and beg' type, I was buffeted from side to side by the crosswinds and dirty air from lorries and cars. Not much fun at all. Plus, it made my backside ache like it had been set upon by the headmaster's cane.

In the end, I elected to sell my mid-life crisis machine and stick to four wheels.

Why? Because I just never felt safe at speed. The acceleration was fantastic, but if you can't hack the speed you accelerate to, there really isn't any point in accelerating there.

Find out how fast you can go. What's your safe speed. By all means, push yourself, as we can all stretch from our comfort zone, but be aware of your own limitations and accept them.

Whatever speed you feel comfortable at is the right speed for you - no faster, no slower. What I want you to be able to do is get there as quickly as possible with the least amount of resistance so that you can meet your potential and achieve your stage and ultimate goals.

3. KNOW YOURSELF

Personal Audit

Sinead had been feeling a little lonely at the weekends. It's not that she had no-one to spend time with. She had plenty of friends. Most weekends, she would meet up with at least one of her three closest girlfriends and their husbands, or people from her running club. It's just that at 38 years old, while everyone else was married or had a special someone in their lives, she was single. She looked at her friends enviously - for the fact they had someone to return home to each evening, someone to support them emotionally. A best friend. A partner. Of course, she knew that it wasn't always perfect - she hadn't just woken up to adulthood. But she was a little jealous of that fact too - that despite the ups and downs thrown at them through life, her friends and their husbands seemed incredibly committed to each other.

It was New Year's Eve that had sent her over the edge. While all her friends were having a great and cosy time playing happy families, she was left with Roger, the only other single person at the party. He was nice enough, but there wasn't any chemistry. More than that, he was very quiet and reserved, while Sinead was that stereotypical Irish girl who was as comfortable with strangers as she was with her best mates. From the conversation they'd had over dinner, he came across as quite negative, which was the last thing she was. It *was lovely of Beth to invite him as her 'blind date' so that she didn't feel left out. In truth, however, she'd rather have been alone than be set up with a guy who was so different to her. What had Beth been thinking? Well, he was very good looking, but that's not enough.*

The next morning, as she awoke from a mildly fuzzy and poor night's sleep, she resolved to do something about this singleton state. She wasn't sure whether she wanted children, partly, she suspected because she hadn't met the right guy yet. But one thing she did know was that at 38 her body clock was ticking by, and it wouldn't be too long before it would be too late to have her own. Sure, one day, she may inherit a ready-made family of someone else's if she waited too much longer, but that wouldn't be the same.

Krystel had flippantly suggested she join an Internet dating site, fully expecting Sinead would reject that out of hand. But as the New Year was beginning, it didn't seem like such a bad idea after all.

With a little fear that it would be a waste of time and money, she began to have a look at the various sites out there.

God, there were loads of them, some of which seemed like meat markets. Then she stumbled upon two that took a real matching approach. One, in particular, was focused on personality traits and matching you up with others in a similar grouping, and very importantly, with the same types of interests.

Sinead thought that sounded marvellous and would probably mean meeting more Rogers would be very unlikely.

As she looked at her own profile, and those of the suggested potential partners the site returned, she became more excited at the prospect there was a Mr Right out there. She'd had enough of meaningless fun with a few Mr Wrongs. Now was the time to really understand herself as a person and, with the help of the dating site's matching engine, match that with a new life partner. She resolved to commit to the process so that in 12 months, there would be no Dodgy Roger lurking for a snog at midnight.

The dating website made use of what is called the 'Five Factor Model' (FFM). Easy to remember with the acronym OCEAN.

The five personality traits are **Openness** to experience, **Conscientiousness**, **Extraversion**, **Agreeableness**, and **Neuroticism**, each with a host of sub-traits. Each of these dimensions is on a scale. Someone high on the extraversion factor (as an example) is very outgoing and energetic, whereas someone on the other end is likely to be solitary or reserved.

There is no sense that a higher level of a dimension is better or worse than a lower level. Being sensitive is not better or worse than being secure (neuroticism). Being easy-going isn't better or worse than being efficient and organised (conscientiousness). We can make use of this scale to help work out who we are and how we respond, which in turn enables us to define an acceleration plan that fits our profile.

The important thing is to find out where you are on each scale so that you can put the best actions in place to help you achieve the goals you've set for yourself.

This is where you need to cast an objective eye over your own personality dimensions and your motivators.

The great news is that there are plenty of places you can get a personality profile done for you (even without having to join a dating site!). Armed with this, you'll know what factors to accentuate and what to work on evolving.

Openness to experience

This scale shows where you are between being closed, cautious and consistent, or inventive and curious. Someone at the lower end of the scale will tend to be conventional, have traditional interests, prefer familiarity over novelty, be quite conservative and resist change. At the higher end, they'll be intellectually curious, creative, be aware of their feelings, and be willing to try new things.

Conscientiousness

At one end, people will show a marked self-discipline, aim for high achievement and be dutiful in completing what they see as expected of themselves. They are more likely to be planned and organised. At the other end, however, is a tendency to be care-free and easy-going, even to the point of being careless. These types will often have no regard for what others expect of them. Interestingly, there is a correlation with life stages for this dimension. There's a rise in conscientiousness in young adults and a decline as they get to older-age.

Extraversion

This is probably the factor where most of us have a view of where we might sit on the scale already. We've spent our lives interacting with other people to one degree or another. Unsurprisingly, extraverts enjoy interacting with other people, have high energy, tend to feel energised by being with others and external activity and situations. They are likely to be action-oriented, enthusiastic, positive, talk quite a lot and be reasonably assertive. By contrast, introverts tend to be less involved in the external world, needing less stimulation from it and more time alone. They can be quite deliberate, quiet and reserved. They are usually good at generating their own energy to get tasks done, without the need to feed on the energy of the outside world.

Agreeableness

We all have to get along with other people in life, but some of us are more naturally inclined towards social harmony than others. Those who are agreeable are usually kind, generous, considerate, helpful, trusting and willing to compromise. They are much more likely to be optimistic, particularly relating to their view of human nature. At the other end of the spectrum, you'll find awkward and disagreeable characters, who are not particularly helpful and don't pay much attention to the needs of others. They are often highly sceptical, suspicious about people's motives and are unfriendly and largely uncooperative.

Neuroticism

This 'neuroticism' is not to be confused with Freud's notion of 'being neurotic'. This scale is sometimes referred to as 'emotional stability' to avoid this. Those people who experience strong negative emotions, like anger, anxiety or depression are often labelled as emotionally unstable. Very often, those with high levels on this neuroticism scale have a low tolerance to stress and are quick to react to situations which they may perceive as threatening or difficult. They are usually very defensive. The opposite of emotional instability is, fairly obviously, emotional stability, where people are less reactive, tend to be calmer and perceive less threatening external stimuli.

It probably won't surprise you to know that some more boffins have done yet more research into personality traits and success in business. For example, people who score very highly on the agreeableness scale may not be as successful at accumulating income as those lower down. Perhaps they are not assertive enough or with a big enough aspiration to earn more.

Leaders tend to score lower on the neuroticism dimension and have higher levels of openness. They are, however, more balanced in conscientiousness and extraversion.

Perhaps unsurprisingly, people who are high on the extraversion scale seem to have a longer, more positive experience at work, while high neuroticism strongly correlates with work burn-out.

How would you score on each of the dimensions?

The point of doing this is to understand yourself better. Find out how you generally behave in the world - your preferences or tendencies.

Try this for a moment. Pick one of the personality dimensions that is towards the beginning, or the end, of the scale (i.e. not one that is slap bang in the middle). Then cast your mind back to a time when you displayed a behaviour, preference or trait that was different to the score you have just got. I'm sure you have many examples - we all do.

I score pretty close to the top end of the openness dimension, which figures. I get bored quite quickly and like new experiences to stimulate me. I'm always looking for new and better ways of doing something. One minute I'm reading about Buddhism, then exploring NLP, then a real Internet surf to see where interesting articles and links take me. Through doing this, I have found lots of fascinating ideas, concepts, tools, philosophies and facts that I've incorporated into my working and personal life. I'm also a writer, and a musician, both playing and composing. So, it's easy to see how I'd score very highly for this dimension. And yet, I tend to eat the same thing for breakfast every day. I'm quite closed-minded about certain things. I also tend to drive to work along the same roads at the same time every day.

So, you see, it isn't hard to find a few examples where I have displayed (and continue to, every day) the exact opposite of what the test has highlighted. This is the point. We can all display behaviour at all points along the scale; it's just that sometimes we tend to cluster them around one end of the spectrum.

If you are right in the middle of any scale, it means you are neither one extreme or another. It's very likely that you sometimes display some tendencies at each end at various times. I'm bang in the middle between extraverted and introverted. I know that sometimes I absolutely love being with people, talk too much and feed off the energy of the external environment. At others, I crave solitude and time to reflect, to recharge my batteries. I don't tend to favour one over the other, displaying both in equal measure.

There isn't any right or wrong result for your personality test. It is an indication of who you are right now and armed with that knowledge you can change the way you behave. You'll need to break some habits and form others, but it is entirely possible to change. After all, you are very likely to have a different level of each of the dimensions today compared to 20 years ago.

To really accelerate, I'd suggest you need to aim for higher conscientiousness and openness and lower neuroticism scores. Aim for being balanced for the agreeableness dimension, and if it's not your usual or natural preference, a little more extraversion will go a long way to helping you increase your metres per second squared.

If you are overly sensitive, you can definitely learn to be less so, and the next section will help you achieve that.

If you're very habitual, some of the tips in the section on luck will get you to be a little more open and freer.

Or perhaps you are on the easy-going end of the conscientiousness spectrum, in which case the sections on discipline and mental toughness will help you become more disciplined and goal orientated.

Those with a broader circle of acquaintances tend to be luckier and can achieve more with the help of their network, so if you are on the introverted side, the sections on luck and networking are for you.

Emotional vs Logical

One fascinating fact is that the big five traits are not unique to humans. Believe it or not, there is a test called the – wait for it – 'Chimpanzee Personality Questionnaire' (!) that has revealed chimps also display these dimensions. And not only chimps - other species show markers for extraversion, neuroticism, agreeableness and openness. It is only the chimp, however, which shares the fifth dimension with us - conscientiousness. Further evidence that we are basically big chimps with less hair.

In Dr Steve Peters' book 'The Chimp Paradox', he talks about the brain being in three major parts - human, chimp and computer. There are in fact seven distinct parts of the brain, each of which plays a different role, but for the purposes of Dr Peters' simplified model, he focuses on three areas - the Frontal, Limbic and Parietal. He refers to these three as our 'Psychological Minds' and to make it as simple as possible he labels each:

Frontal = Human

Limbic = Chimp

Parietal = Computer

As we form in the womb, two different brains develop independently (Frontal and Limbic, or Human and Chimp). Either of them could run our lives, but as they make connections, they try to work together. The big problem is that they are very different and don't see eye to eye on many things.

The Human is rational and logical. It takes in information and can make balanced decisions based on facts. The Chimp, on the other hand, is emotional and thinks independently of the Human brain. Dr Peters' model says that the human is who you are and that the Chimp is independent. We cannot remove the Chimp but can learn to manage it.

Think of the Chimp as our ancient brain, the one that we used thousands of years ago to keep us safe, fed and warm. It was useful during a time in which we lived in a jungle and where there were dangers around us every day. It would sense danger and enable us to react very quickly, based on an emotional fight or flight response. It perceived potential danger everywhere because there *was* danger everywhere, and those who didn't react on instinct under the control of the Chimp brain didn't survive very long. The thing is that we now live in relatively civilised societies, with laws and common cultures that have largely prevented sudden attacks. The dangers we face day to day are almost none. Sadly for us, our Chimp brains do not know this - they can still react in the same way.

The model is nice for three reasons: First, it provides us with an explanation for why some of us can act emotionally, irrationally or do things that we regret an hour later when we've had a chance to calm down and let our Chimp settle. Secondly, it depersonalises the emotional and irrational side of ourselves. It says the Chimp is not you but is a separate being that you can live with and harness. It is, in NLP terms, allowing us to step into second position and observe the Chimp without feeling that it is wrapped up in our own identity. Thirdly it provides an opportunity to learn how to acknowledge better, manage and accept our Chimp so that we can have a happier, more productive and inner-battle-free life.

The Computer (or parietal) part of your psychological brain is where data is stored. This data can come in from either your Human or your Chimp brains. It is basically a large hard drive in our heads that stores information. It's essential to understand that the Computer is dumb, and therefore doesn't distinguish between Human, logical, or fact-based information, or Chimp-like, emotional information. And herein lies the challenge.

We know that many things we do in life are done on autopilot. We don't have to think about making our heart beat, or breathing, or blinking. We know that if we set our minds to learn something, like the piano, eventually we'll be able to play the piece automatically, our fingers skipping over the keys as if they have a life of their own. When Johnny Wilkinson took the last-minute drop goal in the 2003 Rugby World Cup, he didn't have to think about it - he just dropped the ball and kicked it, slotting it through the posts because he had practised it so many times and his body, his brain, his psyche and his timing were all co-ordinated on autopilot. Now, if you can deliberately learn to do things on autopilot, it figures that throughout your life, you will have accidentally learned certain responses or patterns as a result of your experiences and reactions to them. You will have set up some good autopilots (or habits) that help you to function more efficiently because you don't need to think about how to do certain things, but you will also have learned and set up some autopilot bad habit 'Gremlins' as Dr Peters calls them.

Gremlins are usually not very helpful and can be quite destructive. They are often self-limiting. Imagine someone whose Chimp has always felt under attack from their boss - even when everything has been going fine. Somehow, they are naturally at the higher end of the neuroticism scale and are really quite sensitive, wondering whether what they have done is good enough, thinking about the fact that if they don't perform, their boss may get angry, or worse still they may get fired. It is quite probable that this behaviour pattern, or Gremlin, has been learned over many years. Perhaps as a child, they had a father who was incredibly hard to please, and whenever they did something nice for him, like paint a picture or try to give a hug, he was always too tired and grumpy, admonishing them. Then at school, no matter how hard they tried, there was a teacher who shouted at them for getting things wrong, never seeing that helping the child work out how to get the answers right would be a more useful, pleasant and friendly approach. It'd be easy to see how, over a number of years, this child grew into an adult who was lacking in confidence and naturally felt under attack at the slightest thing.

The good news is that Gremlins can be unlearned through the use of NLP and other disciplines. They have taken years to build up, but they don't need to take years to reduce or eliminate. Reframing can be particularly effective to help reduce these self-limiting Gremlins, and we'll look at that in a later section.

The other piece of good news is that it is your Chimp that is responsible for 100% of the Gremlins in your Computer, and because you have the capability to control them, you can eliminate the storage of any new ones from the moment you start to master your Chimp.

So, how can we master an ancient brain that is many times stronger than our Human one?

Dr Peters' advice is to accept that your Chimp is there and will react from time to time. If you try to wrestle a Chimp, you will lose (in real life as well as in the psychological brain) as they are so strong (plus they have teeth and aren't afraid to bite!). He says that the Chimp is the first part of the mind that receives input from the outside - it is the first filter. The Chimp then makes an offer to the Human about how to react, based on its emotional interpretation. The Human doesn't have to accept this offer - there is a choice to be made - ALWAYS. However, if the Human decides to reject the emotionally based offer from the Chimp, this is where the trouble can start, as the Chimp, being highly emotionally driven, will now be very upset with the Human for being rejected. This is where all your management skills need to come to the surface and be used effectively.

Exercise - assess your own Chimp.

The differences between the Chimp and Human brains are as follows:

Human - Evidence-based, rational, perspective, context, shades of grey, balanced judgement

Chimp - Jumps to opinions, irrational, paranoid, catastrophic, black and white, emotive judgement

Undertake the below three steps to evaluate how strong your Chimp is and your own behaviours:

Think about your thought patterns and reactions in the past year. How often has the Chimp won? Would you say your Chimp is strongly present with you, making itself felt and heard often, or is it pretty well under control?

Now reflect on some situations during the past day and think about a specific one where your Chimp was evident.

How else could you have reacted? What would your Human have done had it not been hijacked? Would your Human reaction have been more appropriate? If you'd managed your Chimp and allowed the Human to react, would there have been a better outcome?

Remember that your Chimp isn't you - it just resides in your head alongside you (the Human). But that doesn't absolve you of responsibility for its actions. In the same way that an owner of a dangerous dog isn't the dog (as in they are separate entities) and the dog has its own reactions that are dog-based, it is still the owner's responsibility to manage them, so they don't bite adults or kill children. I have a friend who owns the soppiest, most lovely Rottweiler, who wouldn't hurt a fly. She has been looked after well, trained well, been given love and exercise, and has been made to feel very secure. A lot of people would label her as a dangerous dog because this breed is very strong and powerful, even though it's not on the banned, dangerous dogs list in the UK. However, from time to time, there are stories of dogs that aren't on the banned list causing serious damage to other people, particularly children. Surely you have to blame the owners for not nurturing and managing their dogs, just like we all can and need to do with our own Chimp, from time to time.

Managing your Chimp

Step 1: Nurture the Chimp

Don't ignore it. Nobody likes to be ignored, and it's foolish to ignore something so primitive, emotional, and that's five times stronger than you are. You will fail if you ignore your Chimp. Instead, recognise that the Chimp lives in your head, whether you like it or not, and that it has needs, just like we do. Just like smart people at work make sure their boss is happy, because they'll get less grief from them and may even get a better bonus at the end of the year. And how successful couples actively seek to make their partner happy so that there are love, harmony and a lot more love. We need to make sure our Chimp is happy.

Chimps can feel insecure - if so, go and find out the information needed to make the Chimp feel secure again. They may be quite aggressive or assertive and so participating in a contact sport like Rugby will help to fulfil that need. Some Chimps have the nurturing or parental need, which is fulfilled if you have children, but if you don't, a pet could be a great substitute. Some have a strong need for their own space or territory, so if the scope of responsibilities for a task is unclear, they may react emotionally, in which case, you need to clarify roles and responsibilities, so it feels like it knows where it fits.

Just be smart in making sure that you, as the rational Human, undertake what is necessary to keep your Chimp satisfied. In the long run, this will help you reduce the destabilising effects the Chimp can have on your life and make managing it easier when it does flare up from time to time (which it will).

Step 2: Manage the Chimp

Dr Peters provides three ways in which Chimps can be managed: Exercise, Box or Banana.

A. Exercise

I don't know if people still use pressure cookers these days, but when I was growing up, it was what all the potatoes we ever ate were cooked in. The heat would build up inside, steam would come out of the top and then you'd put the big cap thing on top and let the pressure build-up. As it did so, the potatoes cooked faster than if you just boiled them. They didn't taste great though, being half disintegrated and floury. The hole in the top of the pressure cooker is important for maintaining the correct pressure inside. Steam can escape. Now imagine what would happen if the steam couldn't escape and the pressure continued to build up, and up, and up. Eventually, the pressure cooker and potatoes would explode in your kitchen, covering your SMEG fridge, the beautiful, new, and frightfully expensive KitchenAid and AGA.

That is what happens if you put a lid on your Chimp when it has something to express. The very best thing you can do as a sensible, logical and rational Human is to let the Chimp have a bit of a rant. Let it blow off steam. Vent. Get it all out.

Don't answer back. Don't tell the Chimp it's wrong. Don't tell it off. Don't try to stop it. Just let it fly.

One word of caution - only exercise your Chimp in a safe place and with a safe listener. That means not venting at work, in a public place, at a policeman, at the 83-year-old who unwittingly cut you up at the traffic lights. It means doing this in private with someone who will listen but NOT engage with or indulge the Chimp.

Dr Peters suggests that most Chimps take about 10 minutes before they are all ranted out. After the rant is over, they are more likely to listen.

B. Box

Once the Chimp is quiet, the Human can talk to it with logical, factual and truthful statements. The Chimp has offered some solutions as part of the rant (like revenge, violence, sending a flame email, abusing a defenceless old lady) and it is up to the Human to decide which of these is worth pursuing (if any) and suggest alternative approaches.

These have to be logical, factual and truthful, otherwise the Chimp will not accept them and may flare up again. You also cannot just tell the Chimp not to react, or not to feel that way, as these commands won't fly either. A reasoned response will be much more effective.

"The old lady who cut me up didn't do it on purpose. She probably didn't notice me there. No harm was done. No damage to the car and it didn't delay me at all. I may also make a mistake like that when I'm in my 80s so we can show some compassion. After all, we don't know whether she was distracted because a friend had died, or a grandchild is sick. It's reasonable to forgive her."

Your Chimp is only going to be satisfied if your arguments are strong enough, so be prepared for it to raise its head again and get agitated.

C. Banana

TVs with the picture on but the sound off in pubs, cafes and business receptions is the adult equivalent of a piece of string dangled in front of a kitten. Whatever sensible thing we have been doing up to that point, like having a conversation with our companion, or thinking about the project we're working on, vanishes because there's this thing with moving images on it over in the corner. 'Oh look, a picture of a Hippo. Now an earthquake. Tasty newsreader. Flashing images. Ooo oo oo football!' The kitten can be forgiven because it's a….kitten. We really should know better, but even though that's the case, we still get distracted.

And so it is with our Chimps. We can distract them like a 'terrible two-year-old' who's screaming the supermarket aisle down with a snack. In their case, bananas are good.

This distraction technique can help deflect the behaviour for a short time, but just as the two-year-old will start screaming again once their Farley's rusk is finished, so too our Chimp will eventually finish or tire of the distraction. As a distraction then, use it sparingly or in emergencies.

They can also be used as powerful rewards, according to Dr Peters. If you don't feel much like doing something, telling your Chimp that they can have a reward once you've completed a set of tasks can see it jump to action straight away and help you get focused. Great rewards for Chimps are praise and approval, as well as bananas. They love it, so as a motivator you can schedule time to show your boss what you've done, or show a friend your new oil painting, or invite friends around for a home-cooked meal. Praise and approval from your boss, friends, family and loved ones are the equivalent of tickling your Chimp under its chin while saying, "Who's a clever little thing then? You are. Yes, you are."

I've devoted quite a bit of space to this one model from Dr Steve Peters because I believe it is so powerful. Olympic gods like Sir Chris Hoy and Victoria Pendleton have credited Dr Peters with enabling them to achieve their Gold medals. Victoria Pendleton even says, "Steve Peters is the most important person in my career", while Chris Hoy has said, "Without Steve, I don't think I would have won gold in Athens in 2004".

What I have provided you in a little over 2,500 words is a very high-level outline of some of the fundamental principles contained in his truly excellent book "The Chimp Paradox - The Mind Management Programme for Confidence, Success and Happiness". I thoroughly recommend you read it from cover to cover as it will improve your life significantly. In fact, I think it is so useful that I often buy it as a gift for people.

Accept Where You Are Now

There's an Irish joke that goes like this:

> *Paddy stopped cutting the hedge as the big car drew up beside him and an English visitor enquired,*
> *"Could you tell me the way to Balbriggan, Please?"*
> *Paddy wiped his brow.*
> *"Certainly, sir. If you take the first road to the left? No, still that wouldn't do? Drive on for about four miles, then turn left at the crossroads? No, that wouldn't do either."*
> *Paddy scratched his head thoughtfully.*
> *"You know, sir, if I was going to Balbriggan, I wouldn't start from here at all."*

And, lest I offend any Irish readers, there are many other versions on the same theme. The Two Ronnies did a sketch like this, and both characters were English!!

Stereotypes aside, it serves as a good illustration for a really important point - you must fully accept where you are as you start your acceleration. It's no good wishing you had more time or thinking you should be better at a skill than you are, or that if you get into the right place first, then you'll be ready to start. All of these will lead to frustration. You don't have more time. You aren't any better than you are at that vital skill right now. And there is no such thing as the 'right place' from which to start.

The right time to start the process of accelerating towards your goals is *right now*. It is always right now. The competence you have, the time available, the access to funds, the ability to multitask, the discipline and the motivation levels you have, are what you have. Wishing you felt more motivated, or that you could type at 80 words a minute because that would mean you could write your book faster, or that you had £10,000 of seed capital for your business idea, when you are, in fact, not feeling very motivated, can only type at 20 words a minute and have only about £1,500 in savings, is about as sensible as getting frustrated that you didn't win the lottery last Saturday, when you didn't even buy a ticket.

Accelerating in a Ferrari is a joy. 0-60mph faster than your hair can cope with. Perfect engine, gearbox, aerodynamics, traction. A Ferrari is like a toned thoroughbred, where everything is bred to perfection. If a Ferrari wanted to write a book, it would laugh at your 80 words per minute aspiration. Motivation pumps through its electrical system from the heart of a prancing horse. And your seed capital is the loose change the Ferrari's owner turfed out of their trouser pocket as it was causing an unsightly bulge.

You and I are probably not that much like a Ferrari. I'm more Morris Minor. You may be a bit Skoda. Or Estate car, gas-guzzling Chelsea tractor or hairdresser's car. Whatever you are, there's no point in wishing you were a Ferrari. And that's a good thing. You will probably run for more miles before breaking down. When you go to fill up with fuel, you'll be better off than Mr Sparkly. And believe it or not, when you accelerate any passengers you have with you will feel a lot better than those in the Italian rocket.

I was driven back from London once by my flatmate in his Nissan Skyline (GTR). Not quite a Ferrari, but almost as quick off the line. He insisted on hanging back from the car in front along the Westway and then gunning it until he was virtually climbing up the exhaust pipe of the unsuspecting Renault Clio, before slamming on his oversized carbon fibre brakes. Then he'd do it again. And again. And again. By the time we got back to Ealing, I was ready to taste my lunch for a second time. It was all very impressive, but it was just stupidly quick. And stupidly quick things tend to make even sensible people quickly stupid. My flatmate was an excellent driver, but I couldn't help wondering just how long it would be before he made a howling mistake and ploughed into the Clio.

It's just better to accept that you are as you are. You might be a little slower off the line than others, but you are just as capable of getting to the end (i.e. your goals).

But that doesn't mean you have to settle for what you have, know or are capable of. This process is all about accelerating towards the goals you set yourself. A significant aspect of accelerating is knowing who you are, what you have and looking to improve continuously. Even a Morris Minor can have a souped-up engine, carbon disc brakes, a reinforced chassis and a whizzing turbo. It'll never be very aerodynamic, but even so, with all of those added, it will dramatically increase the acceleration.

You are where you are now, with the skills, capabilities, attitudes and drive that you have. Start with it and build incrementally until you can do what you want to do.

Weather Analogy

It would be remiss of me as a Brit to fill so many pages without bringing up the weather. Let's face it, the weather in the UK is a bit shit.

The Brits will watch the weather to see what's in store, ever hopeful for something good - a barbecue summer, a dry bank holiday weekend.

Britain is to the east of the Atlantic and north of the Azores high. This means we are going to get rain, wind, cold, more rain, lots of clouds, more wind, rain, a bit of sun, some more rain, a bit more cold and a little more wind.

Complaining about the weather is possibly one of the most pointless things any of us can do. It's like complaining that gravity stops us from floating around the house, or that we drown in water as our lungs don't work like fish gills. There is absolutely nothing we can do about any of these things.

But think about this - Britain is one of the most fertile places on the planet. We have green and pleasant lands, woods, leaves that turn from yellows to greens to rusts, fields of barley, corn, wheat and the distinctive yellow rapeseed that signifies it's summer. We have plenty of water, despite hosepipe bans, and enough food to feed everyone. We have beautiful wildflower meadows leading to babbling streams, beaches of pebbles or sand, and rugged rocks and cliffs that have been carved by the stonemason forces of the wind and waves.

Compared to so many of our 7 billion neighbours we have so much to thank our weather for.

Yes, it is pretty annoying when it pours with rain during the annual two-week camping holiday to Skegness or Cornwall.

But complaining about the weather is pointless.

When setting sail for a new destination, a skipper and crew will listen intently to the shipping forecast as their lives may depend on their ability to react. But they don't complain. They choose the right sails and the best course, and then they make sure they have the right amount of provisions and a few options for stop-off ports along the way if the weather turns really foul. Then they go out and adapt continually to all the wind shifts. The aim is to reach their destination safely. Complaining about the weather, or indeed anything along the way doesn't help them achieve their goal in any way.

So, when you feel you're on the edge of complaining about something, just stop and remind yourself that it's like the weather.....no point in complaining. Just adapt your course and focus on getting to the destination.

Reduce bad stress

Are you dressed for success or stressed for success?

Stress is a fact of human life, and it's something that we all need a little bit of. Some measure of stress is what will get us out of bed in the morning and keep us motivated during the day. We need some of it to achieve the things we want and have a fulfilled life.

The issue comes when there's either too much of it or too little. Too little and we are under-stimulated, become lethargic, and it can lead to a crisis of purpose. Too much and our bodies react physically, preparing us for the flight or fight response.

If you're a runner or do any kind of sports, you'll know that you're putting stresses on your body. Muscles stretch and contract. Bones flex under the loads you place on them. There's a certain amount of 'give' in your joints to absorb the transfer of forces. Now, if you harbour an ambition to run a marathon, you'll undertake a training programme to improve your stamina and distance, and every time you go training, you'll be changing some aspect of your physiology. The point is that you are intentionally pushing a little more physical stress through your body each time you train so that your muscles and bones strengthen, you increase your ability to carry oxygen around your system and you improve your time or distance.

We are conditioned to think that stress is a bad thing, but in physiological terms, it isn't. Stress is applied, and the body modifies to be better able to cope with those stresses. There is indeed an optimum range - if you put too little stress through your muscles and bones, you'll get weaker, whereas, too much will cause strain. And it is either sustained partial strain or sudden catastrophic strain that causes physical injury.

There are 3 phases a muscle can go through - the toe, the elastic region and the plastic region. When a muscle is relaxed, it is a bit like a strip of plastic that's been folded multiple times into a zig-zag. If you pull the ends of a zig-zagged piece of plastic, it will lengthen, allowing you to take up the slack. This is what happens to your muscle when you gently stretch it.

The elastic region is where you go a little beyond full length, and the plastic stretches a little, but when you release it, it returns to the same length it was before. You can do this to your muscle by taking it through the toe and then stretching it a little more for 10-15 seconds. You won't do any damage, but you will stretch it a little, which can help you perform your sports better, and if you do it little and often can create permanent changes in the body as it lays down more muscle fibres to cope with this gentle stress.

The plastic region is altogether more troubling. At some point in this zone, your piece of plastic, or muscle will reach the point of ultimate failure, tearing to a point where it will no longer revert to its original length. Do that to muscle and it both really hurts and will take a pretty long time to heal properly. This is stress to the point of strain.

The point is that a certain amount of stress is necessary to help improve your physique and fitness. Don't train, and you simply will not be able to complete your marathon. Train to the point of strain, and you won't even get to the start line.

It's not about eliminating stress that we need to focus on. It is about reducing the wrong type of stress while controlling and harnessing the right type.

In Tim Ferris' book 'The Four-Hour Workweek', he talks about distress and eustress. Distress is the negative type that can injure, and eustress being the good stress we all need - to grow, improve, keep motivated and put down new muscle or habits.

While this physical exploration of stress and the impact on the body is both interesting and provides a great analogy to point to the fact that we actually need good stress, what we really mean when we talk about being stressed relates to psychological, often difficult or negative emotions or mental ill-health.

Psychological stress manifests itself in very physical and often debilitating symptoms. Let's first of all, look at what is produced as a reaction to stressful situations.

At the base of the brain is an area called the hypothalamus, and it reacts to stress by stimulating the body to produce adrenaline and cortisol.

Most of us probably know what adrenaline is. If you've ever watched a medical or hospital drama, you'll hear them talking about administering it to some trauma patients. Who can forget Uma Thurman having it injected directly into her heart in 'Pulp Fiction'? We all talk about the adrenaline rush we get from exciting or dangerous situations (skydiving, roller coasters, seeing the blue lights flashing behind you on the motorway). A first kiss. The fear of public speaking. The thrill of going on stage to perform. All of these situations will prompt your body to produce adrenaline, resulting in a faster heart rate, higher blood pressure and more energy. I bet you that no matter how tired you were before the first kiss from the boy or girl of your dreams, you suddenly felt full of energy. You can thank Mr or Mrs Adrenaline for that.

Then there is the other hormone. The 'stress' hormone - Cortisol. It releases glucose into the bloodstream so you can run away fast or stand your ground and fight. It will also cause other normal bodily functions to become suppressed. It's as if it is funnelling all energy to where it is needed by switching it off elsewhere.

If you have an encounter that stresses you once for a short period, your body will soon regulate itself and get back to normal. Speaking in public once will be stressful (if that's what scares you), but if you then don't do it again, you'll be just fine. It's just like stretching a muscle into the elastic zone - once is OK. No doubt uncomfortable, but OK. More often and you'll quickly get to the point of 'ultimate failure' in the plastic zone.

Unless, that is, you look at the reason you reacted like that. Don't forget, your body's release of adrenaline and cortisol is a reaction to a stimulus or situation. It stands to reason that it's an appropriate response if a sabre-toothed tiger is eyeing you up for lunch, but if it's anything that isn't life-threatening, it really isn't a beneficial reaction.

The good news is that we can all do something about our reactions by *reframing* our thought patterns, building a different map of the world and learning new habits.

Let's consider Barry and Darren. Both are sales reps at a carpet warehouse outlet. They are both good salespeople, but Barry is happy while Darren is often sick.

Barry is always smiling and laughing. He loves his job, and his customers love him for his warm personality and sense of humour. When he loses a deal, he doesn't take it personally. It's just life. It doesn't even enter his head that other deals will fail just because this one did. He doesn't fear for his job, because he knows that each deal is like a mini battle in a much larger war of the 'carpet king' and sometimes it's necessary to lose a battle to win a war. He sees it as a bit of a game, with serious opportunity to earn excellent commission, but his attitude is that you win some and lose others. And when he loses a deal, knowing that sales is a numbers game, he just thinks he's one opportunity closer to the one that's going to close.

Darren, on the other hand, is always worried and stressed. He operates in the same environment as Barry and has access to the same number of opportunities. Indeed, he actually closes about as many deals a year and makes roughly the same money. But he's always highly stressed which is causing him to have problems sleeping. He's not eating properly, and he's moody and fearful. He's had to take time off work because of it, which has made him even more stressed. A vicious cycle if ever there was one.

Despite Barry and Darren being in the same environment as each other, with equal opportunities, they both bring a different set of experiences, personality traits and map of the world. When they were born, neither of them had any map at all, but over the years they've learned things, built pictures in the mind about how the world works and created patterns of behaviour which are consistent with their beliefs.

If Darren has learned the way he behaves, can he un-learn and replace these behaviours with something else?

The answer is yes, and in the sections on habits and reframing, we'll discuss what Darren could do to change the way he reacts.

What's the Evilest Word?

Be careful, because this word is so evil it is barely printable. It is a word that has caused so much guilt, re-crimination, blame and mental torture. It seems so innocuous on the surface - like it's just an ordinary word. It lurks in our language, uttered by people daily. If it could talk to you, this word would tell you it's a meek and mild, cassock wearing, god loving, innocent and angelic chorister with a voice as divine as pure life-giving breath. In reality, though, this word is more like Damien from 'The Omen'. Evil.

Should

The word 'Should' is one of the worst words in our language.

I have no doubt there are a hundred words that you think are worse than 'Should', so let me show you why it's so bad.

Should is rigid. In that regard it sits alongside its equally sinful cousin 'Must'. Should is also a negative word. Think about it in comparison to the word Could.

Should conveys judgement. A teacher who tells a pupil who hasn't done terribly well in a test that they should have studied harder is applying a negative judgement. They are saying that they don't think the child studied hard enough. An overweight person who has embarked on a weight loss programme with the intent of a new, healthy eating regime, may say to themselves that they should eat healthily all the time. We all know that none of us eats healthily all the time, so it is most probably impossible to achieve, and by saying they should eat like that all the time, they are setting up a judgement for when they fail to do so. This, in turn, can turn into guilt, guilt into anger, anger into frustration and, finally, self-blame.

Take a sportsman who tells themselves that they should be able to run an average per kilometre of 4 minutes 30 seconds. When they have an off day because their legs are feeling a little heavy, or they are running a 10km distance rather than a 5km, which needs them to run a little slower in order to have the stamina to complete the distance, and they average 4 minutes and 47 seconds, what do you think the reaction is likely to be?

"I'm a good runner. My average never slips below 4.30. I should have been able to do that, but I failed. I should have been able to complete it. It's so frustrating. I'm annoyed with myself. I'll have to train harder as I should be able to do that. I mean it's not even close to my personal best."

Judgement. Command. Frustration. Guilt. These all the senses we get from the word Should. Negative. Negative. Negative.

Instead of allowing ourselves to descend into this negative thinking pattern, we can choose to embrace Should's saintly stepbrother 'Could'. 'Could' or 'Can' are full of hope, possibility, options, choice, and empowerment.

Think about the situations above and replace could for should.

You could have studied harder (yeah - I probably could have).

I can eat healthily all the time (but sometimes if I don't it's OK as no-one is perfect).

I could average 4 minutes 30 seconds if everything goes according to plan (but if I'm a bit off that because my legs feel like led today that's OK, as I'll have recovered later in the week to try again).

See the difference? Try it the next time you put pressure on yourself over a goal, something at work, or your personal standards. Just replacing two little letters with a different one makes all the difference.

Then there's the almost as evil step-brother '**Must**'.

Imagine you're about to give a presentation to a panel of interviewers for the job you really, really want. It's the last hurdle before you are taken on as the new VP of Business Development, a role that would really accelerate your career significantly. To get the job, the presentation needs to go really well as the competition is fierce.

You can tell yourself the interview 'Must' go well. It can't not go well. It has to be the best interview ever. You must nail the intro, and the graphics must work correctly as you've spent a lot of time on them and they really show what you can offer.

With all of these 'Musts', you put yourself under a tremendous amount of pressure. You are adding to your stress levels. Your palms are sweaty, and your mouth gets dry. You feel shaky. When the projector doesn't work to start with, you feel out of control, as your mental map before the session was that they 'Must' work. You fumble your intro a little and already start to beat yourself up on the inside that you didn't meet the standard you'd set yourself, of 'Must' nailing the intro.

Many things in life are outside our control, so it isn't reasonable to put so much more pressure on ourselves, adding to the stress levels so significantly. It can be tough to do this, but when faced with any really important situation, like the interview, we can change out the word 'Must' and replace it with 'Might'. Just that small change will have a significant impact. That small change in the word will help you change your own mental map and significantly reduce your stress levels.

You can reduce this bad, extra stress. You might even be able to eliminate it altogether.

The Stress Test

In June 2011, the BBC launched an experiment to look at trigger factors for anxiety and depression. They wanted to understand whether biological, social, circumstantial and psychological aspects were triggers and what the relationship was between them. Thirty thousand people completed the survey making this study one of the largest ever carried out into mental health.

The study showed that bad life events as well as a family history of mental health issues, low-income levels, relationship challenges and poor education all factored strongly as predictors of anxiety and depression. But what was more interesting was that those with a strong level of 'adaptive coping' were less likely to suffer than those with lower levels.

Adaptive coping is essentially an individual's ability to cope with what life throws at them — the ability to adapt and cope with the inevitable hardships that we all have to endure.

Those surveyed were asked how they responded to stressful situations. There were four areas covered:

- Undertaking dangerous activities
- The use of positive coping strategies
- Rumination
- Blame

Clearly, undertaking a dangerous activity at any time can be dangerous! When stressed and anxious is can be more so. Of course, hitting the bottle is a path that some take, and it was considered in this category. You might argue that alcohol isn't such an evil that it should be classified as 'dangerous' but taken to excess we all know it can be. And habitually anxious and stressed people can rely on it as a crutch.

Being positive, or trying to be, on its own isn't quite as useful as putting in place some positive strategies. The best ones to keep you from increasing anxiety and heading towards depression are to talk to others about the challenges and to problem-solve. The phrase 'a problem shared is a problem halved' is quite true and can be incredibly helpful. I had a boss once who modified it to 'a problem shared is a problem shelved' - he took it one step further and is never downbeat or stressed. Problem-solving will give you (and a friend) an opportunity to assess the extent of the stressful event and allow you to come up with practical things to do to negate it or alleviate the worst effects.

The two areas that consistently showed up as the ones that contribute to anxiety and possible depression are Rumination and Blame.

Rumination is thinking. Brooding. Going over and over the problem. Dwelling on the difficulty. Focusing on the challenges. It seems obvious doesn't it, that if you let yourself constantly negatively think about things, you're more likely to influence yourself negatively. Ruminating on problems is going to set up a negative spiral of anxiety that will surely fulfil the prophecy, causing untold additional anxiety and self-blame.

And speaking of blame, this is the other big one. Those that look for someone or something to blame for bad situations can cause themselves to become more anxious and depressed. Blaming others is bad enough, but when it turns inwards to become self-blame, it can become incredibly destructive.

The study points to a few things we can take away. First, how we think has a massive impact on our mental health. Negative thought patterns or dwelling on the bad and blaming others can send you into a depression. And secondly, that some things can be done to change the pattern. For instance, there are therapies such as CBT (cognitive behavioural therapy), as well as approaches such as mindfulness.

With knowledge comes a bit of empowerment, and so, the simple fact that you know this, means you can start to spot when your thinking patterns are starting to push you towards a greater level of anxiety than you need to endure. Making sure you share challenges, problem solve and maintain a positive outlook around your stresses while avoiding the crutch of the sauvignon blanc, and the blame or rumination games can make sure you stand the best chance of being prepared to accelerate along your path towards achieving your goals.

Think Stress is Bad for You and It Will Be

Is stress good or bad? It's easy to assume it is bad for us, yet as we saw earlier, it can be an excellent thing. In fact, it may even be necessary.

Evidence suggests that thinking stress is bad for you can shorten your life.

In a study carried out at the University of Wisconsin published in 2012, 30,000 adults were monitored over a period of eight years. They were asked how much stress they had experienced, and whether they believed stress was harmful to health. After analysing this data and correlating it to the public death records, they discovered something very interesting.

People who had experienced a great deal of stress over the preceding year, but who did not view stress as harmful to health didn't show an increased risk of death. Of those who had experienced a lot of stress and did see stress as harmful, there was an increased risk of dying by 43%. Not only was there an increased risk of death in this second group, but those that didn't see stress as harmful actually displayed a *lower risk* of death than people who hadn't experienced much stress at all.

The study seems to point to the fact that what you believe about stress can materially change how your body reacts to it.

Kelly McGonigal, a Stanford University psychologist, started to look into whether changing the thought patters about stress could change the way the body responds. She had spent many years telling people that stress was the enemy, when in fact, that was quite probably the worst thing she could have done. Investigating further, she came across a Harvard study which conditioned participants to view the normal stress responses as beneficial. Instead of seeing the increased heart rate, shallower or faster breathing, sweaty palms and the inner voice as negative, they were taught to view the symptoms as their bodies getting energised and prepared to meet the challenge.

Psychologically they believed that breathing faster was good as it was getting more oxygen to the brain. That their heart beating fast was a positive thing as it was ensuring adequate blood supply to the muscles, and oxygen to the brain. They felt less anxious and more confident just because they had taught themselves to think differently about stress. They had successfully *reframed their thinking*.

These psychological changes also had a significant impact on their physiological responses. Instead of their blood vessels constricting, which is typical for someone experiencing a high degree of stress, they were relaxed. They were basically normal. This relaxed state of blood vessels, along with increased heart rate and breathing is generally associated with states of happiness and joy.

There's another factor to consider in reducing your stress levels, and that is social contact. When stressed, one of the hormones released is Oxytocin. It drives us to be more social and crave support from those around us. The more support we get, the more oxytocin is released. It has been dubbed the cuddle hormone, as it is released when we cuddle someone. It can both stimulate us to seek support and is released when we get the support we need. Oxytocin is a great friend to the heart, too, as it helps repair the heart from previous stress-induced trauma. If you like, it strengthens your ability to cope with stress in the long run.

Is there any evidence that social contact can reduce the risk of dying from stress? In another study by the University of Buffalo, 1,000 adults were tracked and asked both how much stress they had experienced and also how much time they had spent helping their friends out. Again, public death records were used to determine any correlation.

Those who didn't spend time helping others showed a 30% increased risk of dying. Those who did spend time helping those around them displayed a 0% increased risk of dying.

There are two lessons from these studies:

1. How we think about stress affects our response to it and ultimately our risk of early death
2. Reaching out to people for support, or to help them, reduces our stress response and our risk of premature stress-related illness

Make the Next Better Than the Last

Who can forget the one and only hit called (prophetically enough!) "The One and Only", by 19-year-old Chesney Hawkes? In March 1991, this one-hit-wonder burst on to the charts, spending five weeks at the No.1 spot. Its success can be ascribed in large part to the fact it was from the soundtrack to the film "Buddy's Song", which starred Hawkes in the title role alongside Roger Daltrey. Then, with little more than a whimper, the one and only Chesney disappeared from our screens, radios and Walkmans.

Although some people have used Chesney as the butt of their humour, he's done quite well for himself in life, popping up from time to time on various reality TV shows, reliving his hit over and over again. It must be with a mixture of pleasure and irritation for a singer/songwriter, that his one hit song was actually written for him by someone else - Nik Kershaw - and not by his own fair hand. He's released five other singles in the UK but never achieved higher than a 27, and at the worst, hit a depressing 74 in 2002.

I'm not taking anything away from him. I'm sure that every time he puts pen to paper and releases another song, he's trying to do the best he can. In the music industry, it is often not the best songs or artists that make it, but the ones who are lucky, hardworking, have the right contacts, or just have something unique about them. It is often a case of the right look, sound and vibe coming along at the right time for the music moguls to invest in, promote and create a fan base for. The music 'industry' is hard to make work for yourself - there are too many other things at play.

We can take something from the title of the song at least.

If you set yourself a target or a goal to achieve something and you reach these aims, don't sit back afterwards and simply say "I did it". Sure, you can celebrate. You should celebrate. You will be proud. Your friends and family will be proud. You can be satisfied, knowing you achieved something you never thought possible. You can be immensely pleased. But, when the euphoria or hangover has subsided, sit there and ask yourself "How could I have done it better, faster, more effectively?". Ask yourself how you can improve even more.

When I set myself the task of losing weight and getting fitter, my aim was to run 5km. I thought that if I could do that without stopping, then I'd have achieved something pretty significant. And I was right. My first run was a little over a kilometre, and I almost died at the end of it. Yes, five of those would be super impressive. As I continued making progress, I ended up hitting my goal, and aside from being bloody knackered, I was ecstatic. My calves hurt, my lungs felt like a carpenter had sanded them from the inside, and my heart was beating harder and louder than a bass speaker at the Ministry of Sound. I had achieved a km split of 6 minutes 18 seconds.

Two days later I went for another run and wondered if I could run the same distance in a split of 6 minutes 10 seconds. Every time I went out, I aimed to reduce my time by a fraction. Then I found I was achieving a split of 5 minutes 22 seconds. I pushed the distance up to 10km, and my times slowed down - but that was OK. Gradually I improved and eventually was able to run for 10km at a split of 4 minutes 49 seconds per km.

If you'd even suggested that I'd be able to do that ten months before I'd have laughed. But with gradual and continuous improvement every day, the distance had increased, and the split time decreased. Oh, and in the process, I lost just under two stone in weight - all because I was focused on continual improvement of my running technique.

I could have sat down after achieving my 5km goal and sang "The One and Only", but I didn't want to rest, because I knew that there was considerable room for improvement.

In Japanese culture, there is a philosophy known as Kaizen. The word literally means "good change" but is commonly used to refer to the continuous improvement of processes. In the workplace context, it is a daily philosophy that seeks to make work less hard, eliminate waste and increase productivity. Small improvements are made to every area on a continual basis so that, over time, productivity is increased due to a reduction of wasted time and inadequate processes. Toyota is famous for its practice of Kaizen, making it a very productive and 'human' place to work, as it requires teams of people to collaborate in order to implement the necessary changes.

This philosophy doesn't have to apply only to large corporations. Imagine if you had a 'Kaizen mentality' about everything you did. Imagine if you could make a fraction of a percentage improvement to every area of your daily life. What would it do for you if you could reclaim 5% of the time it takes you to do all the tasks demanded of you every single day?

That's over 20 minutes saved during an 8-hour workday. Or, what if it was 10% you could improve by in most areas, by a whopping 40% in one particular area, just by changing the usual way you are used to dealing with it? Perhaps you could save 90 minutes.

Or rather than thinking about time, how about continually improving progress? Focusing on getting more accurate in your touch-typing course by a fraction every day or improving the quality of your communication so that people understand exactly what you're asking of them, so you don't have to repeat yourself and chase them continually.

And then there's one of the most significant areas for continual improvement - management of the ever-increasing deluge of emails at work. Perhaps there is a better way you can manage them that takes less time and is more efficient? I'd bet large amounts of money that most of you could claim significant productive time back by managing email differently.

So how do you continuously improve and avoid your successes and goals being "The One and Only"?

First, create a plan...it always comes down to planning first! What is it you want to improve? If it's your cooking ability, then plan your menus, plan what you need to shop for, plan the preparation and cooking times into your schedule. Make sure you have the right utensils and environment in which to create your MasterChef experience.

Then, do it. That's right, actually do whatever it is you have planned to improve.

Next, check whether it is an improvement. Ask your family what they thought of the meal (hopefully they will be honest). Ask yourself if you managed your timings between courses well. Could you have done with a little more seasoning? Were the dauphinoise potatoes a bit too fatty?

Lastly, act on the feedback and adjust what you do next time. Feed it back into the plan for next time around.

P = Plan
D = Do
C = Check
A = Adjust/Act

It's straightforward. Like many things, it is almost too simple to mention; however, like most simple and useful tools, most people don't embed them in their daily lives.

Can you adopt a 'Kaizen Mentality' or a 'Kaizen Habit' daily? Or will you be happy for each goal achievement to be 'The One and Only" time you reach success, even if that one time it was only at 60% of your potential?

Those who create a 'Kaizen Habit' will accelerate themselves towards peak performance faster. Remember to plan, do, check and adjust….

Body Language

Watching other people is a great pastime. At a cafe, on a train, at the airport. Looking at how people interact and behave is fascinating. Trying to work out whether people are feeling happy, stressed, powerful, unwell, or carefree. The interplay between couples gives away a lot. From those who look like they are in love, to those who are just friends, all the way to married couples that you just know are still together because of apathy.

Body language shines a bright light into how someone sees themselves in relation to their surroundings and others. It also points to how they are feeling deep down.

When we're feeling good, confident or powerful, we naturally stand taller, put our hands on our hips, or generally make ourselves larger. Anyone who has ever won a running race, or something similar, will no doubt have raised their arms up in celebration. This is a gesture that is present even in those who were born with no sight. It is an instinctive, natural reaction that hasn't been learned.

When we're feeling weaker, powerless, unwell or unconfident, we tend to round our shoulders, fold our arms and legs and make ourselves smaller.

Amy Cuddy, professor and researcher at Harvard Business School, has been studying nonverbal behaviour and has seen that there are gender differences. Typically, the men in her MBA classes will come in, sit in the centre of the room, spread out and raise their hands sharply when they have something to say. Women, on the other hand, seem to make themselves smaller, sit around the edges of the room and raise their hands in a barely noticeable way. Of course, there are exceptions to this observation, but in general, it seems to be the case. In Sheryl Sandberg's book 'Lean In' she talks about how women tend to sit at the ends of the table or even against the wall when there are too many people to fit around it. She urges women to *lean in* and take a position at the table.

There is evidence that sitting at the table isn't enough. In a study of the TV programme 'The Weakest Link', contestants standing at the central positions in the semi-circle reached the final round an average of 42% of the time and won it 45% of the time. Merely being in the centre can positively impact your results. Another study asked participants to choose a candidate for a business internship from 5 candidates in a photograph. Candidates at the centre of the picture were chosen more frequently than those at the edges. On that evidence, it would be wise to take a seat at the centre of the table, always.

Cuddy and her collaborator, Dana Carney from Berkley, have shown that our nonverbal behaviour determines how others perceive us. In her excellent TED talk called 'Your body language shapes who you are', she tells how Alex Todorov from Princeton has shown that judgements made from seeing the faces of political candidates for just one second predict 70% of the outcomes for US Senate races. It is clear that people pick up facial expressions subconsciously, process these and make a gut-instinct judgement.

If others can judge our nonverbal behaviours so quickly, what about our own ability to judge ourselves? Professors Cuddy and Carney also wanted to understand whether our behaviours can determine how we feel. There was already some evidence that they can, going back to the 1980s. In what is now a famous experiment, Fritz Strack got two groups of people to hold a pencil in their mouths. One group had to hold it using just their lips, while the other group were only to use their teeth without any of their lips touching it. Both groups were asked to judge how funny they thought Garry Larson's 'Far Side' cartoons were. The group that had held the pencil in their teeth only found the cartoons much funnier than those using their lips only. Why should this be? Try putting a pencil in your mouth (across your face like a dog eats a bone) and holding it in your teeth without your lips touching it. You'll find you are using the same muscles to do that as you do when you smile. Conversely using just your lips will cause you to frown. The evidence showed that forcing your muscles into different positions meant experiencing the feelings associated with them.

To test this further, Amy Cuddy had participants provide a saliva sample, then one group adopted a high-power pose, while another adopted a low-power pose for two minutes. They were then asked to rate how powerful they felt and allowed to gamble before providing another saliva sample.

From this simple experiment, they found that of those who had been in a high-power pose for just 2 minutes, 86% gambled, whereas only 60% of the other group did.

The saliva was used to measure the levels of testosterone and cortisol before and after the 2-minute poses. Those that had been in the high-power poses had a 20% increase in testosterone (which explains the increased risk tolerance and gambling) while those in a low-power pose had a 10% decrease. The inverse was seen for cortisol levels, rising 15% for the low-power pose group and dropping by 25% for the high-power pose participants.

Those with higher testosterone and lower cortisol levels were more assertive, confident and comfortable, while the other group were more stressed and closed. In just two minutes, doing nothing more than taking on a high-power pose, you can change the chemical balance in your brain and change your behaviour.

The bottom line is that deliberately changing your posture can help you feel much more confident and portray much more positive nonverbal behaviours. Give yourself those two minutes before every important interaction, be that a business meeting, job interview, lunch with the in-laws, delivering a speech, performing music or drama, before a sales call, or whatever it happens to be.

The 'Power Pose' in Action:
1. Write down your current feelings about a task you're not looking forward to and note down your posture
2. Watch Amy Cuddy's TED Talk at https://www.ted.com/talks/amy_cuddy_your_body_language_shapes_who_you_are (20 minutes)
3. Stand in the 'Power Pose' for 2 minutes (time yourself)
4. Visualise and feel the best outcome for a task ahead and what triumph will feel like (Optional)
5. Now write down how you feel about the same task from step 1 and note down your posture.
6. Compare the feelings you had before and immediately after adopting the 'Power Pose'. What has changed? How different do you feel about it?

Choose Your Attitude

Have you ever noticed that your attitude can play a massive part in whether something is easy or hard? Whether it takes no time at all or seems to be interminable? Sometimes that task you're being asked to do is one you just don't see the point in, and you kick against. You think it's ridiculous. You are just being asked to do it for the sake of it.

Attitudes can change. Attitudes are chosen.

There are plenty of synonyms for Attitude: point of view, view, viewpoint, vantage point, frame of mind, way of thinking, way of looking at things, school of thought, and so on. They all stem from the way in which you/we see the world and the position we take. The full definition of Attitude is 'a feeling or opinion about something, especially when this shows in behaviour'.

Feelings and opinions can also be changed. Feelings are emotional responses to stimuli, which we label — for example, feeling afraid, feeling upset, feeling happy, sad, cross or lazy. Then, next time you feel scared by something, feel what it's like. Heart beating faster. Adrenalin surging through your system. A heightened state of alertness. Same, or at least a similar thing but with a different label.

Feelings can be changed by changing your mindset. Changing your attitude from one of negativity, looking for the worst, to positivity and seeing things as possible and even enjoyable.

In November 2001 Debra Searle (at the time a Veal) and her then-husband Andrew set off in a race to row across the Atlantic in a home-built plywood rowing boat. They were the only mixed and married crew out of the 36 entrants. They had trained hard for the event which was to take them from Tenerife west to Barbados, a distance of 3,300 nautical miles. It would take the fastest crew a total of 42 days to complete. While they had trained hard for it, learning how to row, how the boat worked, how to make freshwater from the undrinkable water around them, and how to live on it, they had only done so on the river Thames at Putney. There are at worst little ripples on the river, enough to sink an Oxford or Cambridge rowing Eight, but not enough to upset a boat designed to roll with much larger waves and stay intact.

This oversight meant they were unaware that Andrew suffered from a crippling fear of the open sea, so much so that he was physically and emotionally unable to continue. Andrew was rescued from the boat, but Debra took the brave decision to 'row it alone' for the remainder of the trip. She wanted to complete her dream and had been, in contrast to Andrew, loving it out there

It took her 111 days in total, for most of it alone save for her satellite phone and some marine life for company.

During her time alone, she had to row a boat designed for two people, navigate, cook, and do everything else needed to remain safe and on course. Sleep deprivation became a challenge. Her positive attitude started to descend into one of negativity. Christmas came, and she was upset to be alone, away from friends and family. She got to a stage where she wasn't drinking enough. Having initially been quite upbeat and guarded about her real feelings in messages home, she became more open, eventually providing some candid updates to the many, many thousands of people who were following her progress across the world. She received messages of encouragement, which helped. Debra took control and decided that if there was only one thing she could control, it would be her attitude. She'd heard that the achievement of anything is 15% skill and 85% attitude, so she set about developing strategies to keep her attitude right. She wrote those three words on the bulkhead of her tiny ply-wood rowing boat, so she'd see them all the time 'Choose Your Attitude'.

She and Andrew were not the only crew where one member had to be rescued. Other crews, all-male, had a crew member taken off for one reason or another. The only single rower to make it to Barbados was Debra, a woman. So much for being the weaker sex!!

Debra is convinced that the difference was down to her conscious decision to *Choose her Attitude* every day. Perhaps the fact that no other single crewed boat made it to the finish line is testament to that truth.

I encourage you to read Debra's book 'Rowing it Alone'. She became one of my heroes at the time of her crossing, and although they say you shouldn't meet your heroes for fear of being disappointed, I'm delighted that I got the opportunity at an event.

Define Your Purpose

You're reading this book because you want to perform better and accelerate your achievements towards a goal, or because you want to learn how to do that once you've set one. We'll look at the importance of goals and their process steps in a later section, but before we dive into that, can I ask you why you're setting a particular goal (or are thinking about doing so)?

There's a difference between what you'll get as a result of achieving the goal and the reason for the goal in the first place. They may be the same, which is good, but they aren't necessarily.

For example, when I took up running, I wanted to get fit. That was the purpose, and that's what I got. But I also got a lot of other things too. More energy, better sleep, a smaller waistline, better diet. When I extended my goal to running a marathon, it was quite different. Yes, I got fitter and all those other things, but I also often felt fatigued, was pretty hungry most of the time, had ankle and knee pains, needed to spend more money on running shoes and protein powder.

Running a marathon is really hard. It isn't twice as hard as running a half marathon. Your body runs out of energy at the famous 'wall', and you have to dig deep to keep going. The average person is not built for running 26.2 miles. At 6ft4in I know I'm never going to be an ideal marathon runner (boffins have determined the optimal height and weight for running good marathon times, and I'm just neither of those!). If anyone had said I should run just for the sake of doing one I'd have struggled. So along with my goal of completing London, I set about anchoring it to a purpose.

For me it was raising money for the NSPCC, knowing that every stride taken in the difficult period from miles 20-26.2 was helping a child. For others, there were myriad reasons. The London Marathon is the largest mass participation sporting event fundraiser in the World. As a friend once described it, 'it's like a sea of humanity coursing through the streets of London'. Pictures of loved ones who are sick, or favourite charities pinned on their running vests indicating who and what they are running for. It felt like everyone had a purpose in being there. Yes, the egotistical goal of running sub-4 hours or sub-3 hours, but so much more than that besides.

In your specific goals, it will help if you define the purpose behind them. In living your life, it is also the best place to start.

Who do you want to be and why? Simon Sinek is an author and speaker whose books 'Start with Why', and 'Find Your Why' look at organisations and teams and show when there is a purpose first, the rest follows. He uses the example of Apple, which as a business has clearly started from a core principle of what their purpose is and from which everything else follows. Their purpose is their guiding beacon and defines how everything else is done. Simon argues that individuals and teams that focus on their purpose, actively choosing it, establish a guiding principle that colours everything they then do, and how they do it.

If you start with why and define your purpose in your life and goals, then the things get tough, as they inevitably will, you can trace back to the original purpose and remind yourself why.

There's science behind it too. What you do and how you go about doing it are logical and functional. You can draw up a plan for what and how. You can follow it without question if you have to. There's a part of our brain that deals with logic called the neocortex. The limbic system, the ancient part of our brain, deals with emotion, feelings, trust. It's where your inner chimp lives. If you can agree with your inner chimp what the purpose is behind everything you do, then the actions undertaken by the more logical part of the brain will more naturally follow.

In defining your purpose, you anchor yourself to it, and it can become a self-perpetuating cycle, reinforcing itself over and over again.

If you establish that your purpose as a teacher is to enable girls and boys to make a positive contribution to the world, then everything you do will be geared towards that purpose. Engaging with the children will be easier and more meaningful. It will act as a guiding light to help bring children, or yourself, back on course. You'll want to provide the extra encouragement to a struggling pupil; you'll be happy to spend a Saturday or three during term-time running extra clubs, or taking a week away from family to chaperone and look after a group of children on a school trip designed to inspire and open their eyes.

My purpose in writing this book is to help people achieve what they want to more quickly and effectively and to realise more of their potential. My purpose in my personal life is to be present for my family, jointly nurturing the girls to be independent, strong women who believe they can be who they're capable of being (and maybe hoping they'll look after us in old age too!).

When running a sales team, my purpose is always to enable my team to achieve the best work of their careers to date.

Think about yourself and answer these questions:

- **What is your work purpose?**
- **What is your life purpose?**
- **What are your goals' purposes?**

Write them down. Define why you're doing them or being them.

4. BE LUCKY

Luck

Have you ever looked at someone else and thought "How lucky they are"? I know I have. It's usually a manifestation of a little jealousy. How lucky they are to have so many wonderful friends. How fortunate that their marriage is so strong. How lucky are they that their children all got into Oxford? How lucky that he drives an Aston Martin, and she has a thriving business.

The thing is, you can bet almost any amount of money that some of them probably look at you and wonder how you're so lucky in some regard. It's human nature to look elsewhere and see a bright and colourful image where the grass seems a little greener. In reality, they may appear to have so many wonderful friends, but they could still feel a bit lonely. Have you ever been surrounded by lots of great people and still felt alone? Their marriage may look solid to the outside world, but behind closed doors, it's falling apart slowly. The kids might be very talented, but there are plenty of challenges elsewhere. The Aston is probably in the garage being fixed more often than it's driven, and the business could be on the brink of collapse.

Or everything really is wonderful. Who really knows? Who cares?

Someone I knew once told me, "You know sometimes the grass *is* greener, but if you look up, you'll see there are hundreds of birds in the tree shitting on that ground, fertilising it. Be careful where you stand my friend. There may be a very good reason why your own patch of grass is just perfect." To this day whenever I catch myself thinking the grass is greener elsewhere, I always look up and start to assess whether there are any birds, and if there are, whether that's a bad or a good thing.

Comparing yourself to others isn't helpful. Even if things are wonderful and going really well for other people, it isn't some sort of cosmic luck that has made them successful, popular, clever, or resilient.

Luck is wrongly thought of as being something random. As if some people are born lucky and have a guardian angel that gives them good fortune at every turn, when others, yourself included (or so you may think), are destined for the leftovers.

Professor Richard Wiseman became fascinated by the concept of luck, and so began to study what it is, and how it might work. Over a number of years, he conducted many experiments to determine whether there were things that so-called lucky people do to create their luck.

Yes! You read that right…they **create** their own luck.

How about that? What if you could create your own luck to help accelerate your performance? The great news is that you can.

But how does it work?

There are three main ways in which lucky people create their good fortune:

- Optimism
- Intuition
- Openness

Optimism

Mike is pathologically optimistic. Everyone who knows, or has ever met him, says the same thing. Just last week, I saw a mutual friend for lunch, and we got on to the topic of energy radiators and drains. Those people that either suck the life out of you or those who boost your energy, simply by being in the same room. We agreed that Mike is a radiator. Somehow, he is always cheerful, never seems to lose his cool, always has a smile, and is a mine of interesting stories. And the thing is, his circumstances are no different to the rest of ours. He has a tough job that demands long hours, teenage kids, a mortgage that really is too big, and things don't always go his way.

Yet, Mike manages to see the future as a positive place, where things will be fun, good and happy. And where any challenges that come his way will be overcome. Sometimes I wonder how his wife puts up with such constant cheeriness - every day!

If Mike were put in solitary confinement for ten years, he'd emerge at the end with a big grin and tell us that it wasn't that bad really - how it had given him the opportunity to learn more about ancient military history, and how he's grown partial to eating cockroaches.

Mike was definitely born full of optimism, but if you weren't that lucky, how can you change your luck by becoming more optimistic? What are the characteristics of optimism, what can be done to improve them, and how do lucky people manifest their optimism?

What is optimism?

The word optimum comes from Latin and means 'best'. Optimistic stems from this and is typically used to describe an expectation that the best will result from every current or future situation. Most researchers in this area agree that optimism is likely to be a biological trait, but that it is debatable whether it's hereditary. There is some agreement that the degree of optimism has something to do with environmental factors, indicating that it is a largely learned trait.

There are thought to be different explanatory styles of optimism, ranging from depressive pessimism, through defensive pessimism, to realistic optimism, and blind optimism. Martin Seligman, Psychologist, ran an experiment with swimmers, some of whom displayed an optimistic outlook, and others a pessimistic one. After they had swum, they were told their times were a little slower than they actually were. When they then swam again, what do you think the results showed?

There was no change in the pace of those who were optimistic, but for those who were pessimistic in nature, they swam *more slowly*. The hypothesis is that those of a pessimistic disposition are likely to feel that there's little point in trying as hard since the result won't be so good.

And yet, should everyone who has pessimistic tendencies be doomed to underachieving? The answer is no. Other studies have shown that those who display defensive pessimism may, in fact, outperform optimists, because with this trait a complex set of cause and effect arguments can drive them to practice more and try harder in order to beat the anticipated poor outcome.

Certainly, being a blind optimist with no grounding in reality or pragmatism won't get anyone very far either. I know a chap called James, who is so optimistic about becoming a successful and wealthy business owner. He has all sorts of positive images and quotes on the walls around his desk. He 'knows' he'll be successful at it one day. He dreams about being successful. And yet, what he hasn't done is ground his dreams in the reality of what steps need to be taken to make it happen. There is scientific research that dispels the myth of 'picturing success' as a way of somehow creating success. What James needs to do to become a successful business owner (which he has the raw capability to be) is to visualise the necessary steps to get there, and then actually get up off the chair and do them (nothing beats action for making things happen!).

What can you do to improve your optimism levels?

The research suggests that performance can be improved by changing how you think about past results. As an example, two groups were asked to recall the best and worst events that had happened to them over a month and explain the causes. One group was then asked to provide alternative causes to the outcomes, while a control group wasn't. Over time the first group's explanations of cause became less pessimistic. This provides a clue that changing how we think can have a significant impact on our outlook. Over time, the group taught themselves to be more optimistic by merely looking for alternative causes. The more often something is repeated, the easier it is for it to become embedded as a habit.

One way to improve performance is to attribute negative outcomes to a lack of effort and positive ones to ability. This depersonalises the negative items, stopping you from taking them on as a manifestation of your self-worth, and helps you identify more with the positive factors of your ability. A study of basketball players showed that this small change had a significant impact on their results. Optimism training has also been shown to improve how golfers show persistence in attempting to improve their game.

The most important thing to be aware of is that what we tell ourselves about why bad things happen to ourselves really makes a huge difference.

If you miss your train, you have a choice about how you explain that. You can say that it always happens, or that you can never catch trains on time, and both may factually be correct. If you associate these with your ability to catch a train, you can easily see how you might spiral into a thought process which goes something like this:

"I always miss trains. I can't seem to catch them on time. It makes me late. I seem incapable of doing it right. In fact, everything I try I'm unable to do. What's the point of trying to catch a train on time, as I'm unable to do it?"

It's a pretty mundane and ridiculous example, but it's illustrating the point with something we can all recognise.

By associating the constant train-missing to a lack of effort changes the picture entirely. Instead of beating yourself up for being useless, you can now look at it and ask:

"Did I leave enough time after the last meeting to get to the station?"

"Did I spend too long grabbing a coffee before boarding?"

"Could I have bought the ticket in the morning so that I didn't have to queue at the machine?"

In other words, you give yourself an option to look at the things you did or didn't do, or the effort you put into trying to catch it on time so that you can modify your behaviour and positively change the outcome in the future.

The optimism of a lucky person

Professor Richard Wiseman's research shows that lucky people display several very optimistic characteristics that we'd all do well to copy.

First, they *expect* good fortune in the future. Their positivity about the future is significant. These are people who will drive straight past the available parking spaces at the supermarket car park and head for the area closest to the entrance because they believe they will be fortunate and find a space. Unlike the pessimist who doesn't think it's worth it 'because the front-door spaces will all be taken and then they'll lose the available space they are right next to', optimists expect they'll be lucky.

Imagine the lucky person doesn't find a space near the front door. How would they react? This is characteristic number two - lucky people turn their bad luck into good. As Mr Lucky drives around the car park again, he doesn't dwell on his ill-fortune. Instead, he'll see the positive side of it. Perhaps it'll be easier to get out of the car park if he isn't so close to the door, or perhaps he'll bump into someone he knows in the other part of the car park, or maybe it'll just be easier to load the car up with fewer people, children and trolleys around.

Lucky people are generally sure that any ill-fortune will work out for the best in the long run. This attitude enables them to 'let go' of any negative or pessimistic thoughts. Imagine how liberating that feeling is. No matter how bad things might seem, the belief that things will work out for the best frees them from anxiety and negativity.

I'm sure you have experienced a situation when some things didn't go as you wanted. Perhaps you didn't get the job you wanted, your relationship has ended, or the purchase of a new house has fallen through. While in the middle of these unwelcome events, it feels like they're the most important and negative things. But have you noticed that something that felt like it would cause the world to end ended up OK? In fact, didn't it sometimes turn out better as a result? The job you didn't get was with a company that went bust six months later. The relationship that ended freed you up to meet the partner of your dreams. The house you couldn't buy had subsidence which would have cost a fortune to sort out, and in any case, you found a home to buy that is better in almost every way instead. Very few things are disastrous, and history teaches us that most things do indeed work out for the best. The difference between a lucky person and others is that they have faith and believe it will work out before having to be proven right.

The lucky are likely to take steps to prevent bad luck. Having seen that something has not gone as they'd have liked they will look for the reasons. Then they will work out how to change behaviours or circumstances so that next time they are luckier. With everything we do in life, we can improve the chances of future success by reflecting on what happened and seeking to make changes. We have already looked at continuous improvement in the previous section, so you know what to do, and how to do it. Now you also know that it is one of the fundamental traits of lucky people.

Have you ever met up with someone and thought it'd be a difficult meeting, or that you wouldn't get anything from it? I bet you were right. I'd put money on the fact that you predisposed your meeting to being unsuccessful because you approached it with a pessimistic mindset. Lucky people, on the other hand, expect their interactions with others to be lucky and successful. With a positive and open attitude where they expect good things, they are better able to create their own luck.

Paul is going for a job interview. He's confident of his experience, he knows the details of the company he's seeing, he's done his research about the interviewer, and he's feeling positive. He expects that the interview will go well and that he'll have an excellent interaction with the interviewer. Of course, he doesn't have a clue whether he'll get the job - he'll be compared to the other candidates they're seeing. He knows that job selection is out of his control, but that the interview itself is very much in it. Because of his expectation, he is relaxed and smiling, warm and engaging. When he arrives at reception, he engages the receptionist in conversation in a friendly manner. He greets the interviewer and begins to establish some common ground based on the research he did on LinkedIn. The interviewer responds well to the interest being shown, and they continue to talk so that a natural level of rapport builds up. Then the interviewer starts to question Paul about his background, experience and interest in the company. Paul is able to answer these well because of his preparation and relaxed, engaging style. As the conversation deepens, the interviewer begins to give away some more information, which is useful for Paul to address one of the questions. He spots this and reacts with a much better answer. At the end of the interview, he asks a couple of questions that

make the interviewer think hard before answering as he feels confident and believes the interviewer will appreciate them.

Once Paul leaves, the interviewer reflects on the conversation and feels that he was very natural, engaged and engaging, intelligent, experienced and above all, the right kind of confident. Paul leaves, feeling the interview went as he expected it would - successful. He feels it will be lucky too, and sure enough, he's offered the job.

The final optimistic characteristic is one of perseverance in the face of uncertainty. It's very easy to feel discouraged when things get tough at work or when you're not sure how they'll turn out. When a project seems to be going nowhere or taking a very long time, it's a normal human reaction to doubt whether it will ever achieve the initial objectives. When I was setting up a consulting business, I spent over two months meeting with hundreds of people searching out my first piece of work. Every day I met with up to 6 different people, talking to them about their businesses, and seeing whether, and if, there was something I could do to add value. The initial week was easy - it was quite exciting and fun. But as the weeks went by and I got more worried about whether I'd ever find a paying client, I started to wonder. The mind can play nasty games when you let a little self-doubt in, and sure enough mine started telling me that there wasn't any work, that the evidence that I'd find a paying gig was stacked heavily against me considering everyone I had so far met hadn't needed me. It was then I remembered my sales training from 20 years before when I'd been a door to door perfume salesman.

What a job that was! These weren't even brand name perfumes but were what are known in the business as 'renditions'. They were never sold as if they were the real things, so technically they weren't fake. And they weren't made out of hideous chemicals either. They were real perfumes that were made to smell as identical to the real thing as possible so that only a bloodhound would be able to tell the difference.

Armed with 20 bottles of different fragrances, I would knock on doors of businesses to try and sell them a perfume that smelled identical to the one they already wore. My differentiators were that they were twice the strength and double the size for less than half the price.

If you want a soul-destroying job, you'd do well to apply right now. The number of people who said "no thank you" was small. The number who said something verging on aggressively rude was very much higher. Those who said yes were as rare as hens' teeth. Whenever I found someone who actually wanted to buy one, I would always 'REHASH' them. ***Remember Everyone Has Another Sale Hidden'***....it is much easier to get repeat business from someone who has already committed to buying than to get another hundred rejections. The hidden sales could be a present for their mum, girlfriend, cousin, or maybe they want to smell nice with a few different fragrances - a different one for every day of the week.

I ended up being very good at it and was promoted to running a distribution centre, which meant that I had to train others to start on the commission-only, hard, hand-to-mouth sales route of rendition perfumes.

The path was as uncertain as you could get. Every day started from scratch, with the sales clock set to zero. I couldn't plan what kind of people I'd meet, or the number of units I'd sell. All I could do every day for myself, and for the new recruits I was coaching, was to remain optimistic and persevere in the face of uncertainty.

I trained myself to look at rejection as an excellent thing. Rejection was my friend. In any sales role, you chase opportunities, many of which don't turn into business, some of which do. To a greater or lesser degree, perfume sales is a maths conundrum. The more opportunities or prospects you chase, the higher the probability of making a sale.

Knowing that for every 20 people who told me 'where to go' there would be a sale, I knew that after the first rejection I was one person closer to delighting a customer with a cheap, large, strong-smelling bottle of a fragrance that they actually wanted to smell of, and in turn, pocket the cash.

I would walk around chanting 'So what? Next!' while making a mental note of how close I was to the sale.

And so, with my consulting practice, 20 years on, I applied the same thought pattern. I reframed my thinking so that it became a positive experience each time I bought someone lunch or a coffee and they didn't want to use me. And sure enough, less than three months after starting on the consulting journey I had three new clients and a whole set of different problems - how to squeeze eight days' worth of work into an average week.

Of course, I approached that challenge with as much optimism, and sure enough managed to complete all three projects on time, while delighting the customers. How lucky is that?!!

How optimistic would you say you are? Very. In the middle. Not at all?

Answer the ten questions below to find out where you sit on the scale.

For each question, assign a letter from A-E, based on how much you agree or disagree with the statement:

A = I agree a lot
B = I agree a little
C = I neither agree nor disagree
D = I Disagree a little
E = I Disagree a lot

Take the test:

1. In uncertain times, I usually expect the best
2. It's easy for me to relax
3. If something can go wrong for me, it will
4. I'm always optimistic about my future
5. I enjoy my friends a lot
6. It's important for me to keep busy
7. I hardly ever expect things to go my way
8. I don't get upset too easily
9. I rarely count on good things happening to me
10. Overall, I expect more good things to happen to me than bad

Scoring:

- For questions 1, 4 and 10, note down a score of 5 for letter A, all the way down to a 1 for letter E.
- For questions 3, 7 and 9, note down a score of 1 for letter A, all the way up to a 5 for letter E.
- Now add up your score. The closer your total is to 30, the more optimistic you are, the closer to 6, the more pessimistic your outlook.

Remember my friend Mike? I hazard a guess that he'd score an impossible 43!!!

Intuition

Call it intuition, a hunch, a feeling, or a sixth sense. We've all had them. I'm sure you can think of examples where you had a feeling and did or didn't act on it. Did you thank your lucky stars you acted on the hunch, or regret when you didn't?

I was at a career crossroads once upon a time. I'd left my previous job through opting to take a redundancy package. It felt like the right time to go, and being able to walk away with a cushion of cash meant I wasn't under pressure to have to get a new job instantly. I could take my time to assess the market.

While talking to a number of corporates, I worked in an interim capacity for a small video conferencing company. They had been in discussion with a technology firm to license their new and very exciting collaborative video offering. My job was to build the business case to seek equity investment in order to drive the new proposition to market as well as negotiate the contract with the tech company.

That was all going well until I got further into the recruitment process with one of the corporates, which prompted the MD of the video company to discuss joining them full time. Of course, the corporate job would come with a decent package, but with no opportunity to earn above that. The video company were offering less than half, but with significant earn-out opportunity in 5 years.

This was a classic risk vs reward decision, where the upside was potentially huge with this new technology. I modelled spreadsheets to look at personal cash burn scenarios. I talked to friends, almost all of whom were urging me to take the exciting job with the deferred pot of gold.

And yet, I couldn't sleep. I became an insomniac for a few weeks. My brain churning through the upsides of the exciting potential - the chance to build something, experience taking a company through funding, growth and a likely trade sale, potential wealth at the end. My gut was telling me something entirely different. I tried to analyse whether it was just that I'm slightly risk-averse, but that didn't explain the power and strength of the feelings.

I opted to take the corporate job, and instantly, my sleep patterns were restored. My gut settled. I felt at peace for the first time in weeks.

I've tracked the company over the years, and while it's still going, it is still very small. In fact, it is pretty much the same size now as it was then. The technology has been surpassed by slicker, quicker, more readily available, and better-marketed products. They have sold a few contracts to the oil and gas sector, but not in the volumes needed to support the investment or get anywhere remotely close to the potential pot of gold.

I've often thought back and believe the cause of my unsettled stomach was the MD himself. I realised he would never relinquish full day to day control or let the business change as it needed to in order to develop the capability to sell in large volumes. The throttle-neck was him, and I sensed that I would neither be able to work with him nor that the business case would stand a chance with him at the helm. At least one of those has been proven right.

The biggest problem is that intuition can't be explained - at least not scientifically or rationally. It makes it very hard to say how it works or to prove that it exists.

And therein lies the answer - even if we can't explain it, we all intuitively know it exists and works because we've experienced it. The real question is, do we listen and take action?

Lucky people listen to their gut feelings and hunches more often than unlucky people. Another experiment by Richard Wiseman showed that 90% of lucky people trusted their intuition in personal relationships, while 80% listened to it and acted upon it in their career decisions. Overall, 20% more lucky than unlucky people used their intuition in making financial decisions and career choices.

So there is a strong correlation between those who are lucky in life and acting on intuitive hunches.

But is there a way to explain how we might form hunches? And what can we do to improve our intuitive ability?

Many psychological experiments have been conducted to understand the subconscious in order to try and provide a rational scientific explanation for how and why we create hunches. One leading theory is that our subconscious recognises and stores a significant amount of data that we cannot process consciously. In one experiment, a short random sequence of squiggles was shown to participants. The squiggles were meaningless shapes. They were then shown a very long list of squiggles, some of which were the same as those they had previously been shown. They were asked to identify which ones they had seen before, but none of them could - it was just too difficult. The experimenters then asked them to indicate which of the squiggles they liked. The results? The squiggles partici-pants preferred happened to be the ones they had seen on the original shortlist.

When asked why they preferred the shapes they had indicated a preference for, the participants came up with several explanations to justify the decisions. They tried to fit a logical reason for the choice to something that none of them was even aware of - that their subconscious had registered and stored the information, then guided them to make a choice based on something familiar.

Similar results were recorded from other experiments indicating that it wasn't a one-off anomaly.

Based on these findings, it becomes easier to accept that intuition is real and provable. Essentially, when you have a hunch, or 'that feeling', it is because your subcon-scious has picked up information that you are not aware of at a conscious level. The subconscious can process the in-formation and compare it to other data to provide a strong 'guide' to your conscious self.

The trick is to listen to your hunches, never shelve that uneasy feeling, or dismiss what your inner voice is telling you. Always listen - at worst it will make you re-evaluate something, at best it may just save your life one day.

The second thing that lucky people naturally do is find ways to enhance their intuition. They give themselves space to allow the subconscious to process information. It may seem hard in a hectic world to do this, but there are a couple of things you can do to improve.

You could learn to meditate, emptying your mind of all thought. This requires time and patience, but the impact on your life could be more far-reaching than an improvement in intuition. It isn't easy, so rather than give you any specific advice on how to meditate, your best bet is to research types of meditation and take the plunge if it's for you.

The easier thing to do is to take yourself away from the situation for a while - shelve it. This is the one time when you can allow yourself to procrastinate. If you have several options and are having trouble making a decision, write down all the pros and cons of each and then step away from things and do something entirely different. When you come back, you may find that your inner voice is telling you something emphatically, in which case, listen to it. If it isn't, you can pick an option and write a justification for choosing it. Then, step away again and do something entirely different again. The important thing is to do something else - anything else instead of thinking about the decision you need to make. Don't sit there trying not to think about the choices, as that won't work - we all know that if you are told not to think of a pink elephant, that is precisely what you do think about. That's why you should go and do something else for a while, perhaps something creative to exercise the other side of your brain. Then, once you return to the decision at hand, you can take a look at the justification you wrote and let your feelings and inner voice tell you if that really is the best decision.

This may sound like it all takes time, and initially, as you practise building your intuition levels, it will. But the more you do it, the better you become, and the stronger your subconscious will guide you towards a life full of luck.

Openness

It's an immutable law of nature that those who adapt survive, while those who don't die out. Just ask the dinosaurs! Apply it to almost any walk of life, and you see the same pattern repeating itself. Those businesses that stay the same, doing things in the same old way they always did go out of business. If they don't fold entirely, they will find a rapidly changing consumer group taking their business elsewhere, turning them into a much smaller company.

Species that don't adapt struggle to survive. The Vaquita is the world's smallest porpoise. It's very rare and wasn't discovered until 1958 as it is so elusive. It was very happy in its native habitat, the Gulf of Mexico, until commercial fishing started to decimate their numbers. They are caught in gillnets and die. They are classed as critically endangered, and it's believed that there are fewer than 200 left on our planet. Unless humans intervene to protect them, they will die out. There are dozens of species on the critically endangered list and no doubt hundreds of others that are endangered.

Being able to adapt is one of the things that sets humans apart from other animals. Our normal body temperature is 37 degrees centigrade. A 5-degree core temperature drop is considered a medical emergency with hallucinations, delirium, complete confusion and extreme sleepiness that leads to a coma. A four-degree temperature rise is also a medical emergency with fainting, vomiting, headache and dizziness. In a naked state, we have very little to protect us and need a relatively narrow temperature range to survive. Yet, we can live in temperatures of plus 50 and minus 50 degrees quite comfortably. We adapt to our surroundings by adding or removing layers of clothing. We invented air conditioning and electric heaters. We have developed insulation for our buildings that keeps heat out or in depending on the conditions.

When new technology comes along, we adapt and adopt it pretty quickly. Our diets have changed over many years from meat and vegetables to significant amounts of grain, and we have adapted to cope.

We are clever, resourceful, and unlike the poor Vaquita, infinitely adaptable. We are all living proof about just how adaptable the human race is.

While we are all adaptable in many ways, we are not all equally so. Give ten people any situation, and you'll get ten different reactions ranging from totally open, to entirely closed-minded, and all points in between.

In the previous chapter, you will have discovered where you sit on the Openness personality dimension. Were you part of the 11% of the population that sits at the inventive extreme of openness, or the 29% who are quite open and likely to experiment? Perhaps you are part of the 20% that sits somewhere in the middle. Or are you habitual along with 40% of the population?

The evidence of the research into luck shows that those with higher levels of openness are luckier. Through being open to new experiences, they expose themselves to new ideas, situations, people and opportunities, and consequently have a greater number of resources to call upon when the time comes. Those who are very habitual tend to do the same things, in the same way, taking the same route to work, eat the same things, go to the same places. By doing this, the opportunities to expand knowledge, experience, contacts and perspective are much diminished.

If you catch fish in the same river, at the same spot every day, you will only ever catch the same type of fish.

One day, if you pull enough of them out of the river, the numbers will dwindle, and you'll start to catch fewer. If you cast your net in a few different locations, you'll open yourself up to new types of fish, with more abundance. It seems pretty obvious that the more open you are to new experiences, the more information and experience you're exposed to with which you can make both conscious and subconscious (lucky hunch) decisions.

If you are in the habitual or even the average range, how can you work on developing your openness?

Try something new every day. Don't have the same coffee at the same coffee shop. Have a peppermint tea at a place you've never been to before. Drive a slightly different way to work. Run a different route to your usual one. If you usually sit at your desk eating a sandwich every lunchtime, go out for lunch with a different colleague once a week. Or here's a better one - that conference call that you hold at the same time every week - you know the one everyone has to turn up to but hates - well, cancel it and let the team do something else that's more productive instead.

Here's another suggestion. Ask six friends to name something they'd like to do and write each on a separate slip of paper. Then fold each one in half and put into a bowl. Mix them up, close your eyes and pick one. Whatever it is, you MUST do it. No putting it back and choosing a more conservative one. Be open to it as a new experience. You never know, you may actually love it. And it might be the one thing that causes you to have good luck.

We also know from our personality profile that some people are more easy-going than others. On one extreme of the Conscientiousness scale, you have people who are ultra-disciplined, and at the other end those who are easy-going. On the Neuroticism scale at the sensitive end, people are likely to display more anxiety than those at the other, more emotionally stable end.

I would argue that discipline is not the inverse of easy-going, and that anxiety is perhaps a more accurate opposite. It is perfectly possible to be easy-going and relaxed about life but be conscientious enough to be disciplined about your goals, be they work-related or personal. Being neurotic about your goals and discipline, thereby becoming anxious about hitting every milestone, or being fixated on a path to reach them is closer, in my view, to the antithesis of easy-going.

In the end, it doesn't matter too much how they are classified. What matters is that the research indicates that lucky people have a relaxed and easy-going attitude to life. Because they are not overly anxious, they notice things that those with a narrower view may not. Relaxed, easy-going people repeatedly reported that they often stumbled across life-changing information when reading magazines, or surfing the internet, because they allowed themselves time, without a rigid, anxious focus. They had the space to notice things, take them in and act upon them.

The best advice if you are usually a bit uptight or anxious, is to invest some time in relaxing. Meditation may help. Slow, deep breathing exercises can also help put you into a calmer frame of mind. But perhaps the most important thing to do if you are busy and driving to achieve your goals is to schedule some time in the day that's devoted to doing nothing in particular, where you are not focused on your goals or projects, where you are focused on being, rather than doing.

The final thing that lucky people do is develop and maintain a vast network of people around them. They are very good at making those around them, be they long-standing friends, or brand-new acquaintances feel good. They are usually friendly and open to new personal encounters, no matter how brief, and are approachable. Some are even social magnets that others see as dependable, engaging, and fun.

The Extraversion element of your personality profile will give a hint as to your sociability and social skills. If you are already in the top 40%, you likely have a wide range of acquaintances and friends and are very open, perhaps even craving social contact. Those at the introverted end may still have many friends, but typically their social circle is more limited. The important difference is that introverted people generally don't crave to be with other people, and some can even find mixing with those they don't know, or large groups quite tiring and stressful.

Wherever you are on the extraversion dimension improving your interactions with others and building a strong network will enhance your luck factor. Make an effort to be in contact with someone you haven't seen in a while. Every week get in touch with someone different and meet for a coffee, beer, lunch or dinner. Then catch up and talk about life. Exchange information. See if you can help them in any way. Find out about their family and what new hobbies they've taken up. In unearthing this information (and sharing the same level back with them), you widen your experience base and will uncover something that makes you sit back afterwards and think - "it was fortunate that I met up with them again just at the right time".

When getting lucky through your network, be sincere in wanting to find out about others, if possible, finding out how you can help them (helping someone is the best way of establishing trust and a bond), and maintain it.

Don't just call on people when you want something. Stay in contact because you like them and are interested.

The more people you are in contact with, the luckier you'll be.

5. INFLUENCE AND PERSUASION

Influence

Stuart was feeling a bit miffed. His idea was great - at least he thought so. No, he was convinced so! In fact, he knew his ideas were pretty good. Why didn't anyone else see things the way he did? Why was no one else convinced?

Stuart's latest idea was to create a content marketing engine for his company by creating a customer FAQ and then writing about each of the questions a customer might ask. He thought that if he got a team of people from across marketing, product and sales together in a workshop they could brainstorm the sorts of things that customers might want to know, and then allocate out the topics to members of the team so that everyone could participate and be part of a quality content marketing engine.

Simple, right! But his boss and the other stakeholders weren't buying it. He was at a loss to know what to do to persuade them. He wondered if there were any things he could do to become better at influencing those around him.

The great news was that after a few weeks, Stuart returned to the topic again, but this time he'd become a persuasion ninja. And this time, he took a different approach entirely. Over the course of another few weeks, he managed not only to get the stakeholders to agree, but this time they seemed to really want to engage.

◈

Much has been written about the art of persuasion. All backed up by significant amounts of peer-reviewed scientific evidence. Perhaps the most well-known authority on the topic is Robert B. Cialdini PhD, who has written many books, including 'Influence: Science and Practice' and 'Yes! 50 secrets from the science of persuasion'.

What are some of the techniques you can learn to become more persuasive, and that'll help you accelerate your performance in whatever goals you've set yourself?

Technique 1: Remember and use people's names

It may sound obvious, but we all generally like the sound of our own name. Even people whose names we might think sound daft usually like the sound of their own names. In his 1936 masterpiece 'How to Win Friends and Influence People', Dale Carnegie wrote: "Remember that a person's name is to that person the sweetest and most important sound in any language".

How do you feel when you are greeted by name? Most of us may not have thought about it much but think back to someone who always uses your name when they speak to you and how it makes you feel compared to those who don't. When someone uses your name to greet you, or in conversation, it makes the interaction more personal. They have remembered your name, which for a lot of people is really not that easy, and secondly, they are addressing you personally.

If you walk into a cafe or restaurant and are greeted by your name every time, you are going to feel a personal affinity for the place and go back many more times. Not only can it make you feel good and better disposed to people, but someone using your name in a disagreement has the very subtle effect of softening your stance. You won't even notice it, but there is a wealth of evidence that points to this phenomenon.

So, to help build excellent relationships with people and make them feel the interaction is personal, you need to remember their names and then use them.

Beware the fine line between drawing them towards you with the right frequency of use or turning them off with the 'used car salesman' over-use. There is, of course, a reason why the car salesman uses customers' names - the next time you notice someone using your name a lot in conversation you'll know that they might also be an influencing ninja.

Technique 2: Be a copycat

Perhaps it's best not to do that incredibly irritating thing that kids find hilarious by copying every sound, word and movement you make. That thing where you tell them to 'stop it' and they just mimic you and repeat 'stop it'. It goes on until you want to draw blood. No, that kind of mimicry will at best cause funny looks and at worst cause you to lose an eye. It certainly won't help you accelerate towards achieving your goals.

That being said, there is a great deal of evidence, much of which comes from the research undertaken by Richard Bandler and John Grinder in the field of NLP, that shows how mirroring, matching, pacing and leading can help build rapport.

Rapport is essential in any relationship. People who are in rapport communicate better, like each other more, are more receptive to ideas and suggestions, and appear to each other as being 'like them'. If the sweetest sound to us is that of our own names, the next sweetest is to be with people who are like us. Of course, this can be at an obvious level, such as both having a love of carp fishing, an interest in medieval history, or football, but the real rapport building takes place at a subconscious level.

People who are in a state of rapport tend to match their posture and language naturally. When two people are engaged and in rapport, and one leans forward, the other is likely to do the same. Likewise, if one leans back, folds their arms, crosses their legs or takes a sip of their coffee, the other is likely to make a similar type of change. Filming this and playing on fast forward would reveal a dance between the two people - an ebb and flow of movement as they both subconsciously mirror the other's behaviour.

We all use language differently, too. Broadly we break down into three groups, sensing and filtering the world through one of three lenses: Visual, auditory or feeling (they call it kinaesthetic in NLP). We experience the world with all of these senses, but most people have a dominant natural preference out of the three.

If you listen carefully to people as they speak, you should be able to hear whether they have a natural preference. Their language will be peppered with words that give it away. Those of a visual preference will use words like see, picture, imagine, colour, or anything with a visual connotation. Auditory people will say hear, sound, noise, etc., while kinesthetics will say feel, touch, crave, sensitive, grasp, etc. They will also give these clues away in their writing.

To have the maximum chance of building rapport and influencing someone, you need to match their body language and their sensory preference.

The next time you're talking with someone, notice how your posture and body language is in comparison to theirs. If they lean back in their chair or scratch their head, modify your body position too. Whatever you do, don't play the kids game earlier and make it so obvious that they end up stapling your hand to the desk, but do lean back subtly and instead of scratching your head, touch your chin. Once you have established a state of rapport, you can then start to lead them to be more engaged gradually by leaning in, using hand gestures to be more animated, or briefly touching their upper arm.

Nicolas Gueguen is a French psychologist who has spent his career investigating many interesting things, including the effect of women's breast size on men's likelihood to stop to pick up a hitchhiker. The results of that experiment don't even need mentioning - just too obvious! He did, however, also discover that a short touch on the upper arm for only 1-2 seconds can significantly increase the likelihood of a request being granted. Hardly surprising, given his previous research topic, that he chose to experiment in the context of attraction between men and women, however, the conclusions have been tested in more mundane everyday situations and found to be just as powerful.

In his first experiment, he had a young man approach over 100 women in a nightclub over a three-week period. He would approach them, introduce himself and ask if they'd like to dance. With half the ladies he asked, he briefly touched them on their upper arm, but with the others, he did not. 65% of the women he touched agreed to dance, whereas only 43% of those he didn't touch did. In a second experiment, three men were tasked with getting the phone numbers from women on the streets. Almost 250 women were asked, and again with half of them, they were touched briefly on their arm as the chat-up line was delivered, while the other half was unhanded. Double the women who were touched on their arm provided their phone numbers compared to the other group.

Touching someone's upper arm for just 1-2 seconds while delivering a request or making a suggestion is scientifically proven to increase the likelihood they will agree by between 50-100%. I hope it goes without saying that this needs to be done subtly and with integrity or there'll be a risk of a harassment suit winging its way to you.

You can also mirror language. If they predominantly use visual words, do the same. If they write emails with mostly kinaesthetic words, then write back in the same way. In fact, I would go further than that and suggest you should write back in the same style. For example, if they address you "Dear Joe", then reply "Dear Peter". If they use short sentences, do the same. If they sign off saying "Best Regards", or "Yours", then do whatever they have done. I very often finish emails with just "R" instead of writing my full name. When others reply in the same way, I notice, and I think they're like me. If someone is very formal, I'll be formal in return.

It is essentially about giving yourself the best opportunity to build rapport and influence others to help you achieve your goals. People like people like themselves. People like helping people like themselves.

Technique 3: Everyone has to eat and drink

No-one is living on this planet who doesn't need to eat and drink, and at least one of the three daily meals is slap bang in the middle of the working day. I'll bet there are a few coffee machines in your office too or at least a kettle. Use them to your advantage.

Caffeine has been shown to increase people's persuadability by up to 35%. In a study, researchers gave all participants an orange drink and asked them to read a series of arguments on a controversial matter. Half the drinks had been spiked with caffeine; the rest had not. Those who had unknowingly been given caffeine were 35% more favourable to the arguments they had read than those who had only had orange juice.

Of course, not everyone drinks coffee or tea, and those who do may restrict their intake to have more in the morning than the afternoon. Find out if the person you need to persuade is a coffee or tea drinker and then buy them a drink in the morning. They will both be more receptive to your ideas and good arguments (this does not work if the arguments are not very good) and they will be better disposed towards you as you've given them a gift.

Psychologist Gregory Razran found that people who have a meal together are better disposed towards statements, objects, concepts and ideas that are introduced while eating. The hypothesis is that food makes people happier, and therefore, they act more impulsively and quickly. Again, you can go one better than only having a meal with someone, by insisting on paying.

As human beings, we survive based on cultural norms that include reciprocal behaviour. We instinctively understand that interactions are based on give and take, and we like there to be a balance between what we receive and what we give back.

Psychologist Dennis Regan conducted an experiment in which a researcher posed as a volunteer and was asked to rate the quality of paintings in an art appreciation experiment. Along with the research volunteer, a series of other real volunteers were asked to rate the art. Each time the experiment was run, the researcher was with only one other person, one of the real volunteers.

Half the time, during a break for rating the art, the researcher went and bought two cokes, returning to the volunteer and giving it to them as an unsolicited gift, while the other half of the time, he left and returned with nothing. Later in the experiment, the researcher asked the volunteer whether they'd buy some raffle tickets for a car. When the researcher had bought the cokes, the number of raffle tickets purchased by the volunteer was significantly higher than when they returned empty-handed. This experiment demonstrates that by doing someone an unsolicited favour, you are likely to have a return favour provided back to you. Hence, if you have the opportunity to go out for a drink or a meal with someone you want to influence, pick up the bill.

Technique 4: Many little acts make for a significant impact

There are four parts of this technique, all of which are small, but used together (and with the ones listed above) will provide you with much better results. Master them all, and you can be a black bandana-wearing 'Influencing Ninja'.

1. The first one is an extension of the principle we just looked at from Regan's experiment. The evidence is overwhelming that the rule of reciprocity is very powerful indeed. And it even works if the person you

are doing the favour for doesn't like you. Another experiment was run where researchers sent Christmas cards to a group of random strangers and guess what happened…a very high proportion of these random strangers sent a card back to someone they had never met before. This is how strong the obligations set up by the reciprocity rule are. You have probably 'fallen' for this yourself with those charity envelopes from the Red Cross that give you a couple of coasters, greetings cards and a pen in the same envelope as they ask you to donate money. Did you send them some? I'm sure more of you donated than would have if it had just been a begging letter.

The important thing is that the favour is done before getting anything in return. To increase your chances of influencing, do a small favour without being asked, and do it before you ask someone to consider your ideas or plans.

2. The second technique is to 'get your foot in the door'. One of the six pillars of influence is Commitment and Consistency. The rule effectively says that people like to act in a way that is consistent with their actions or commitments. It is as if there is a giant, cosmic mirror that reflects our self-image. Experiments have been conducted where the effect of a mirror has been shown to increase honesty. At Halloween, an experiment in several different houses tested this effect. When trick or treaters came to the door, the host let them in, showed them where the bowl of sweets was, told them they could have only one each and then made an excuse to leave the room for a moment. In the unmodified houses over 1/3 of the children took more than they were allowed. In the houses where a mirror had been strategically placed so that the chil-

dren would be able to see themselves taking the sweet from the bowl, less than 9% of them took more than their fair share. Having a mirror reflecting our own image can increase honesty because we feel a need to be consistent with the image we have of ourselves as honest and decent.

In the same way, a virtual mirror hangs over every one of us guiding us to be consistent with the decisions, actions and beliefs we have already committed to. In Robert Cialdini's book, he tells how, during the Korean War, American soldiers who were held in prison camps run by the Chinese were frequently asked to make very mild anti-American or pro-Communist statements. They were so mild that you could be forgiven for thinking that they were of no consequence. Statements like 'America isn't perfect' seem pretty obvious since nothing is perfect. Once they had agreed with these trivial points, they were pushed to agree with something a little more substantial, and perhaps write a list of all the problems with America. Then they might be asked to write about it in an essay. The stronger, more detailed and public these statements became, the higher the likelihood that the prisoner would change their allegiance altogether. The Chinese were very effective at getting the majority of prisoners to collaborate in some way by employing very sophisticated psychological tactics.

In another experiment conducted in 1966, two groups of homeowners were approached to volunteer to have a huge billboard erected in their front gardens - one that would pretty much obscure their view from the house. In one group, only 17% of those asked said yes. In the second group, 76% of them did. The only difference between the groups was that those in the second group had been approached before the main request and asked if they would mind putting a small sticker presenting the same message as the billboard in the corner of one of their windows. The fact that they had made this commitment to a particular cause or message had such a dramatic effect on their willingness to have an ugly, view-blocking, full-sized billboard ruining their front gardens.

To help you influence and persuade someone to agree to your project, or to give you help, or buy a product from you, or do what you need them to do to progress, you need to get your 'foot in the door'.

If you are sure someone is sufficiently favourable to your plan then, by all means, ask them to support the whole thing from the start, but if they are neutral or negative towards it, try getting them to make a very small commitment first. Instead of our friend Stuart trying to get the whole content marketing project off the ground in one go, he could first ask the stakeholders whether they think the successful content marketing approach of another company is good. He could ask whether they thought the current content marketing programme is delivering enough of a return - is it working? He could then ask the stakeholder to collaborate with him on putting together a case for why the current content isn't working and co-present their findings and thoughts to the rest of the team. Finally, a pilot could be suggested where the negative stakeholders are asked to nominate a team member to contribute one article to the effort.

You get the picture....it's about taking small steps and getting small commitments, then asking for a slightly bigger one until eventually they have drunk the Kool-Aid and changed allegiance or started seeing the project as their own idea.

3. The third little action is to ask them to do you a favour. Benjamin Franklin was more than just "the First American"; he was an author, printer, political theorist, politician, postmaster, scientist, inventor, civic activist, statesman, and diplomat. He invented the lightning rod and bifocal glasses too. While President of Pennsylvania, between 1785 and 1788, he was having problems with a hostile, opposition politician. Instead of attempting to use flattery or servile respect, he opted for an altogether different approach. He had heard that this man had a very rare and curious book in his library. Franklin wrote to him, asking if he might borrow it for a few days. He received it almost straight away, and when he returned it, he attached a note thanking his hostile combatant very much for his kind favour.

The impact was profound. The very next day, this man spoke to Franklin very civilly and seemed ready to do another favour for him at any moment. The two became great friends until this man's death.

Franklin observed, "He that has once done you a kindness will be more ready to do you another, than he whom you yourself have obliged."

Researchers have subsequently tested what has been dubbed the Franklin effect many times, and the proof is conclusive. That requesting a favour from someone can have a material impact upon their likelihood to do you more favours in the future. It is another example of how someone will end up acting in a way that is consistent with their previous actions.

To help you achieve what you're looking to do, you would be well advised to ask your stakeholders to do you a small favour. This effect doesn't work for favours that are perceived as too onerous. You could ask them to write you a recommendation on LinkedIn (perhaps drafting what you'd like them to say about you first!), or lend you a book, or send you a copy of the presentation they were telling you about, or even join your next team call to speak for 5 minutes on what their team has been up to. The possibilities to ask for small favours are almost unlimited. Just make sure you keep them.

4. The last one is to get them to say "**yes**" three times before you ask them the question you want the real "yes" to.

   Have you ever been in a situation where you've found yourself unwittingly agreeing to something? Have you ended up buying something you never set out to buy, and didn't even really want? Do you want to find out how to get others to agree with you or do something you suggest more often?

   Asking questions, to which the answer is either yes, or positive, before asking for the thing you want agreement to is one of the most effective ways of influencing someone. Politicians do it all the time. Salespeople do it often.

   We know that we all want to be consistent with our previous actions, to the extent that this is a fundamental motivator of behaviour. This need to be consistent has led us to create responses on autopilot, responses that we need give no active thought to. We act automatically in many situations because we have pre-programmed ourselves to the appropriate response. This is a good thing in the main because it means we don't need to think hard about every bit of information that's hitting us every day. For the routine, or things we have seen before, and where we have built a view of an appropriate response, we act or speak on autopilot.

A researcher called Daniel Howard experimented with the effect of getting someone to answer yes, or positively to a question before asking for what he was really after. He called residents in Dallas to ask if they would agree to allow a representative of a charity to come to their house and sell them biscuits to raise money. 18% of those asked agreed. On another occasion, he first asked residents "How are you feeling this evening?", the overwhelming majority gave a positive reply. In this group, 32% of residents agreed to a charity representative coming around. Of the 32% who agreed to a visit, almost 90% of them bought biscuits. The need for consistency is very powerful.

The research has shown that acting on autopilot to give a favourable, positive reply to an innocuous question such as "How are you?" can have the effect of increasing someone's likelihood of agreeing to what you ask them for. The more often the person answers something with a yes, or a positive reply, the more likely they are to be consistent with their positive frame of mind on autopilot and agree to your full request.

Be Nice

When I talk to people about persuasion and influence or about NLP, I'm often greeted with comments decrying them as manipulative or Machiavellian. It's as if somehow those who learn to master these sciences are guilty of inflicting Voodoo on unsuspecting victims, bending wills to their own.

I don't agree. Understanding social science and how people act, react and interact is a very worthwhile activity. What are business, family, or social lives if they are not made up of human interactions? Learning can help all of us understand how things really work, why they tend to happen as they do, and then equip us to modify behaviours in order to improve ourselves and the lives of others.

This suspicion or fear of social science voodoo is really centred around those who try to use these techniques to fool, rob or con. There will always be those who seek to use powerful truths for their own personal gain while leaving a wake of devastation. They start out with a selfish or negative intent.

For the vast majority of us, the intent and purpose in our lives are positive. Setting goals that are positive, enhancing to those around us and ourselves, is what we strive to do daily.

Achieving your goals can be sped up by understanding and utilising the laws of human social interaction and psychology. Just make sure you reflect and ask yourself whether you are harming anyone when you employ these tactics - if you aren't, then use them wisely. If you are, then shame on you, and I urge you to stop right now.

I believe that those who try to use these techniques to bend people's wills against the fundamental core of what they want or believe in will not succeed in the long run. You only need to be duped against your will once to be suspicious the next time.

6. SET GOALS

Set Goals

How many times have you set goals only to realise a few weeks or months later that you're no further towards achieving them than you were when you set them? The classic goals we set every year are usually done so on the 1st January - our NYR (New Year's Resolutions). By January 15th we're in a state of depression - Christmas and New Year are over, and we're still in the depths of cold, dark, miserable winter (at least in the UK). Comfort eating in front of the TV suddenly seems preferable to the diet that was promised after the December gorging. It's too cold outside to exercise, and even the trip to the car to drive to the gym after work, in the dark, seems a stretch too far.

How many of you make yourselves accountable for achieving your NYR, or any goals? How many of you truly commit? Who is going to tell you off if you don't keep to the plan? Who are you setting the goals for?

If you don't set yourself any goals, I bet that no-one cares. Perhaps a family member will think it'd be good for you to get a bit fitter or lose a couple of pounds. Perhaps your spouse pays lip service to your intermittent statement that you want to write a book. But ultimately no-one else cares a damn about your goals, or whether you achieve them.

Don't get me wrong. If you set out to run a marathon, and make it in a good time, I'm sure your friends and family will be pleased for you. None of them is likely to care whether you completed it in 3 hours 30 minutes or 3 hours 32 minutes. The only person who actually cares is you. After all, it wasn't their goal for you to run a marathon in 3 hours 30 minutes - it was yours.

YOU MUST commit to YOUR goals. Commitment means to work towards achieving them no matter what obstacles are thrown in your way.

If I commit to deliver $3m of business to my company in a year, it is my job to ensure I put in place all the right actions and initiatives to achieve that goal. I commit to deliver. And committing to deliver is the same as pledging that I will not fail.

When I was presented with two career choices at one point in my life, a friend told me that 'Commitment is Power'. I realised I was hedging my bets and committing to neither freelance consulting nor finding a new job. I kind of felt that if the consulting thing didn't work, then it didn't matter much as I could always get another job. I also felt that it wasn't a train smash if I didn't get a job as I could always earn money freelancing. The result of this? I wasn't getting another job, and neither was I finding any freelance work.

So, after Paddy's pearl of wisdom, I decided to commit. I had always wanted to try my hand at freelancing, to see if I could do it, to have a change of lifestyle. From the next day onwards, I started to set some goals because there was the reality of needing to generate income pretty quickly.

Following the commitment came the accountability. I realised that I was accountable to myself for achieving success as a consultant. No-one else could assume the responsibility for the actions and outcomes I needed to attain. No-one else was going to make sure that the things that needed to be done were done.

If I failed to do what needed to be done, then I would need to take responsibility for that, look myself in the mirror and apologise. I would need to man up and assume accountability. I would need to look at my daughter and apologise that there wasn't any food on the table and that she wouldn't be having a summer holiday.

Nobody, other than me, could be accountable. At its most basic, accountability is finding a way to do what needs to be done, no matter how many times you may need to do it, or hours it may take to complete. It is refusing to fail in delivery.

What do you think is the enemy of accountability? There are a few candidates. Procrastination perhaps. Or lack of resources maybe. I say there is only one - 'Excuses'.

If you commit to doing something for someone (or yourself) and fail to deliver it when you said you would you have a choice. You can either face the other person (or yourself) and say 'I failed and there is no excuse. I will remedy it urgently and make sure it doesn't happen again'. Or you can say 'I failed to complete it because I didn't get the right support', or '…because something more urgent came up', or '…the dog ate it, Miss!'

The first of these takes responsibility and full accountability. The second one is just a bunch of excuses and demonstrates a lack of accountability. Someone who truly owned the task and saw themselves as accountable would have ensured they got the support they needed or completed the task despite something else needing attention.

Try this for the next few days. Consciously take accountability for the goals you set yourself. Every time you notice yourself giving some sort of excuse for not completing something on time, put a £20 note in a jar in the kitchen. Label the jar with the name of your nemesis. At the end of three days, you MUST give that person all the money collected.

That'll make you feel differently about true accountability.

Well-formed Outcomes

Before setting yourself any goals, take a moment to consider if they are 'well-formed'.

If your goal is to land on the moon, and you're not an astronaut isn't very well-formed. If you are 45 years old, have only just taken up running, and have never run a marathon before, setting a completion goal of under 2 hours 30 minutes is not well-formed.

You're probably more familiar with the concept of SMART objectives. Those that are specific, measurable, achievable, realistic and time-bound.

Specific - Setting a goal that is too general is unlikely to result in success. This is one of the many reasons why every well-intentioned NYR doesn't work. 'Get fit', or 'lose weight' are too general. Be more specific - 'go for a run three times a week', or 'eat a maximum of 1300 calories a day for six weeks'.

Measurable - Define what you are going to measure. How many or how much? How do you know you've achieved it? Don't just say you'll write *some* of your book. Say how many words you'll write each day, and how many days of the week you'll do it for.

Achievable - Is it actually possible to achieve? How will you do so? There is little point in deciding you will send your pet monkey to the moon unless you actually have a pet monkey and a spaceship.

Realistic - Are you willing and able to work towards the goal? Is it realistic at the age of 53 to think you can beat Mo Farah at a 10Km race when your average is 4:55 per km and Mo runs in 2:42?

Time-bound - Don't leave it open-ended. Don't just say you'll lose weight. Say that you'll do it by March 31st, or by bikini and beach time. It needs to be a tangible deadline, not an open-ended nothingness, non-commitment.

What is a 'Well Formed Outcome'? And how does it differ?

Just like all good and memorable models, WFOs also have an acronym. PACER - Positive, Achievement, Context, Ecology, Resources.

Positive - This may seem obvious, but you'd be surprised by the number of people that don't do it. Too many people focus on what they don't want, rather than what they do. "I want to be less tired" is not as powerful a goal as "I want more energy". "I want to lose 12 lbs" is not as positive as saying "I want to be 10st" (instead of 10st 12lb). Always state the goal in the positive. Make it something you are aiming for and travelling towards - not escaping or running away from.

Achievement - How will you know when you've achieved the goal? This is similar to Measurable, above. Make sure you know what you are measuring, what you'd see, feel and hear when you achieve it. Imagining this can help cement the goal and your commitment to it. Ask yourself how someone else will know when you've achieved your goal. Is there something you can show them as evidence?

Context - Not every outcome is appropriate all of the time. For example, if your desired outcome is to be more assertive because you are often overlooked at work, consider whether this outcome is also appropriate when discussing with your spouse whose turn it is to do the washing up! So, when do you want the outcome and when don't you? With whom and where? Context is key.

Ecology - This is about determining what the positive by-products are of achieving your goal - what will happen when you get it? Think about what you might need to give up or lose if you attain it. Check to make sure that the outcome you desire fits with you as a person - is it representative of you and where you're going?

Resources - There's no point setting a goal to get into the local football 1st team if your job involves significant travel preventing you from training regularly or playing in weekend fixtures. You need to make sure you have enough resources (time, energy, money, support, help) to initiate the actions AND maintain them.

While I prefer to state PACER in that order, because I think it is best to start with a positive intention, you can also make the work RECAP from the same letters. Start by being SMART and then RECAP on what you defined. Recapping, or reflecting, on your objectives will turn them from goals into **'Well-Formed Outcomes'** which will stand the best chance of achievement.

Focus on Process Steps or Stage Goals

You know that goal you've always wanted to achieve? That one where you finally own the 36ft yacht. The one where you cross the finish line of the London to Brighton bicycle race. The one where you have your own business and customers are actually paying you their hard-earned money. That one where you become Senior Vice President. The one where you take your new-born baby back home.

Think about the goal. Visualise it. Feel what it feels like to achieve it. What will you hear? What will your friends say? What will you do when you get there? What are the emotions you'll feel in the moment? How will it change your life?

Visualising will help you keep motivated to want it. It'll help you keep focused and pull you back when your attention starts to flag, or other things (like life) get in the way. You should visualise in detail...after all what is a dream if it isn't a visual experience in your head? A great dream can be a completely enveloping experience for all your senses. You know how powerful a dream can be if you've ever woken up in the middle of the night with the sweats from a vivid and seemingly real experience.

Visualising is not enough on its own. You need to work back from the goal. What needs to take place in order to have a baby? You needed to find a partner and one that wants to be with you and have your baby. You needed to build a relationship, agree to have some fun, do a pregnancy test, buy some maternity clothes, take time off work, eat for two, wonder what life would be like afterwards, buy things for a nursery, think of a name, go to scans, go to NCT classes, form a support group with other mums/dads, go into denial, buy car seats and a sensible car, buy a cot, pushchair, clothes, and a papoose (a what?), wait for the due date, wait for it to pass, wonder if it'll ever happen, wonder if you/your partner will ever be the size they once were again, feel the waters break, rush to hospital, get high on gas and air, blame the father for the pain, suffer excruciating pain, have a baby.

Wow, the baby is here at last.

A few days later you take him/her home and, if it's your first, realise that the dream/visualisation of taking them home for the first time was completely and utterly wrong, as panic sets in that you just don't know what you're doing and aren't sure you're quite ready to be this much of a grown-up yet.

While I realise that it's possible to have a baby without all of the above being strictly necessary, the point I'm making is that there are many 'process steps' that get you to the final goal. If you don't define what these process steps are, you're very unlikely to achieve your target. Write them down, working backwards from the main goal and ensure you focus on achieving each one - one by one.

Ayrton Senna did not become the greatest motor racing champion without knowing what the process steps were to get him towards his goal. Lance Armstrong didn't cheat his way to 7 times winner of the Tour de France without focusing on illegal use of blood doping along the way. Luke Skywalker knew he had to focus on mastering the 'Force' before he could save the resistance.

The next time you set yourself a goal, visualise it and then focus on what you're going to have to do to make your baby (real or metaphorical – all your goals are your babies) a reality.

Start and Keep in the Moment

Have you ever looked at your to-do list and thought there's just too much on it? There are some pretty large items, and there are lots of smaller ones too. The large ones seem hard and difficult; they'll take quite a bit of time to do. The smaller ones are shorter and easier.

So, what do you do? It's simple right. Your list has ten things on it. Three are in the large camp, and seven are smaller and easier. Do the maths. If you get the seven smaller ones done, you've wiped out 70% of your to-do list. You'll feel really good about yourself. You're an efficient time management hero. Just look at you, 70% of your tasks completed. Oh yeah! You marvellous creature.

Oh No! Don't fool yourself into thinking you're some sort of Work-God. You may have done 70% of the items on your list, but you've probably only done 10% of the work. Choosing to tackle the easy, smaller tasks first is another form of procrastination — a way of lulling yourself into feeling productive without actually being.

Say that you're setting up your own consulting business. On your to-do list you have the following items:

1. Write business plan
2. Open business bank account
3. Find an accountant

4. Create website
5. Design company logo
6. Print business cards
7. Register for VAT
8. Complete company registration
9. Design value proposition, marketing messaging and collateral
10. Start prospecting

Which ones are the large items? Which are the smaller, easier ones?

I've set up a number of businesses over the years, and I can tell you that items 2-8 are the easier, shorter, more admin related ones. Number 1, 9 and 10 are the meaty ones that will actually start your business. I'm not saying you don't need to do any of the others - you absolutely do. But the ones that take the most effort and time, that are the hardest, are the ones that enable you to define an operating model and plan for your business so you know what you're aiming to achieve, how you'll achieve it and how you're tracking against that (1 - your business plan), define what you're going to sell and how you're going to articulate the value to the customer (9 - your value proposition, messaging and collateral), and knocking on doors and picking up the phone to drum up business (10 - your prospecting activities).

The big tasks are the ones you MUST start with. Start with the most important one, writing a business plan. Why? Because without the plan you don't know what you're supposed to be doing. In effect, you don't have a map of where you're going or the route showing you how to get there. It's the one stepping-stone goal that all the others flow from. If you haven't done this one then you don't know what you're value proposition is, you can't realistically call people to pitch your business, you won't know what to put on your website, and you don't really have a reason to open a bank account, register for VAT or even register the company. You probably don't know enough about what you're going to do to know what to call your company.

But there's an issue, isn't there. A business plan is a large document. It'll take ages. There's research that's needed. You'll have to apply thought and structure. It seems like a mountain to climb. This large, never-ending task stretching out in front of you, when all you really want to do is get a quick sugar fix from registering a website address, contacting Barclays Bank, and filling out the paperwork for Companies' House. But you need to start. Just start it and keep in the moment, focusing on each and every process/stage goal until you've completed the most important tasks.

Marathons are long. I know that the period between miles 18 and 26 are sheer hell. They hurt. Like hell. When I look at a map of London and see the route of the London Marathon, my heart sinks. How far? God, it's a long way. Tower Bridge is still only halfway around the course. It's also a very long time to run for without stopping. I'm not particularly speedy as I have a late 40-year-old body and I'm 6ft 4inches tall. Three hours 55 minutes is a very, very long time to run for.

So, what do I do? If I focus on the whole race, I'd never start. If I focus on the pain of the last third, I'd never start or keep going. Instead, I don't think about the race at all. All I think about is the start of the race. The gun goes off, and I focus on crossing the start line. I focus on my breathing and my cadence. I take a look at my watch to see my pace. I enjoy being part of the event, being part of the 33 thousand strong sea of humanity flowing through the streets. I let the momentum carry me to the half-way mark. I then focus on the specific parts of my race plan to help me through the last 8 miles. What I never do is think about how much further there is to run. I keep my mind in the moment and focus on the task in hand.

Stay in the moment and eventually you'll get to where you're going.

The three most important things to do are:

1. Focus on the larger, more important goals first - these are the ones that'll make the biggest difference
2. Focus on the start - just start something, even slowly, but start it
3. Focus your mind on the task in hand - keep in the present and get the start completed, then get the bit after the start completed, then the next bit, until you're at the end

When writing this book, I'd never have started if I'd focused on the gargantuan task of writing 75,000 words. I'd still be dreaming about writing a book if I'd looked at the 75 sections I'd need to fill spread out into the far distance. I'd probably be moaning about the fact that I have a book I want to write but don't have the time to commit to such a large project.

Instead, I decided I would write a short piece called 'The Problem'. Once I'd done that, I wrote another short piece. Some days I didn't feel like writing, so I didn't. Other days I did, so I did. Then there were the days when I knew I had to in order to hit my deadline. On those days when I didn't feel like it or was tired or too busy, I just focused on the start. I sat down and made myself start writing a paragraph. It didn't need to be a very good paragraph. It just needed to be a paragraph. And on almost all occasions when I focused on the start, by the time I'd written the paragraph, I felt there needed to be another one to illustrate the point made in the first one. Then another to develop the ideas. Then another still to tell a story about the concept. An hour later and a new section was finished, a section that had I not simply focused on starting would never have happened.

Start something. Anything. But just start it. Now.

What Gets Measured Gets Done

A former colleague used to say, "What gets measured gets done". It was one of his favourite phrases and one he passionately believed in. When I looked at the results of his team versus some of the others, I was struck by how much more consistent he was in achieving what he set out to. His team had a better and more predictable business win rate. They had more customer references. They hit their new business goals more often than the other sales teams, and in addition, each member of his team hit the goal, whereas in other teams there would be a couple of heroes who would smash the number every month and a whole lot of people who didn't get close.

When I decided that being 14st was 1st 7lbs heavier than I wanted to be, I measured my progress every day. EVERY day. There weren't some days I didn't do it because I was 'too busy' or just forgot. I committed that I would measure a number of parameters every day.

I set up a simple spreadsheet recording my weight, measured at the same time every day before breakfast. The date was recorded, along with body fat and water percentage. These were plotted on a graph so I could see progress over time. The last part, plotting on a graph was an incredibly easy and important step as it showed the trend. It is too easy to focus on the end goal and then get discouraged because the results along the way are not what we want, so we give up. There were days when my weight increased and other days when it decreased. If I hadn't plotted the trend, I could easily have focused on the increases and thought there was no point. But over time, the graph showed a downward trend, and I could very easily see the impact of the things I was doing to achieve the goal. I also learned to interpret the correlation between hydration levels and fat percentage, so I knew that if I was very dehydrated, my fat percentage would likely be higher, and my weight would be lower. If I was well hydrated, it would be reversed. Having more than one parameter to measure is a good thing. Getting fixated on weight alone is not healthy. Reducing body fat and increasing hydration levels is.

I was keeping score. Whether your goal is to get a new job, start a business, compete in a triathlon, raise money for charity or find a new partner, keep score. Keep looking at your goal and measure your progress towards it every day.

How many interviews have you attended? How many jobs have you applied for? How many companies have you researched, or members of your network have you reached out to?

How many training sessions have you done on your bike this week? How many miles logged pounding the pavements? How is your swimming split time improving?

How many online dates have you been on? How many photos have you swiped left or right on Tinder to look for a date? How many new conversations have you had with complete strangers? How many blind dates have your friends set you up with?

Write the scores against the goals you set using the SMART and RECAP methodology. Measure the progress against each of the process/stage goals too and evaluate how they are going.

In an earlier section, we looked at the difference between the end-result goal and the stage goals. My end result goal was to become 1st 7lb lighter (a positive goal versus the negative one of losing 1st 7lb!). Measuring progress against that goal is a good thing, but guess what? If you don't put in place stage goals and do something towards achieving them, your progress chart will be a flat line.

To become 1st 7lb lighter I decided to do two things; 1) eat only 1,300 calories a day as this is the minimum required before my body would go into 'starvation' mode, and 2) run 5km every other day. A pound of fat is roughly equivalent to 3,500 calories; therefore, I would need to burn off a total of 73,500 calories, give or take a few.

The recommended calorie intake for a man (in the UK) is around 2,500 per day, so I could create a deficit of 1,200 per day, or 8,400 per week, plus running 5km slowly would burn approximately 1,050 calories (350 calories three times a week). I could essentially reduce my weight by 2.7 lb a week if I stuck to my plan. That would mean getting to my target weight in approximately eight weeks.

(NOTE: I am not a doctor and am not recommending anyone eat or exercise at this level. I undertook the specifics of this plan after reading many books and seeking advice from a nutritionist and doctor. Please consult a doctor if you are considering losing weight. I am providing this as an example of how I set goals and measured them in order to achieve my aim.)

To run 5km three times a week was easy to measure and record (a Garmin watch and iPhone app helped a lot). But to eat 1,300 calories a day was going to be less straightforward. The great news is that almost everything you buy from a supermarket has the calorie and nutritional values printed on the packaging (in the UK). It was a matter of discipline to check this information and plan what I would eat every day. A small bowl of cereal in the morning. A salad with plenty of green, healthy stuff and some protein or soup at lunch. A proper balanced meal in the evening.

It was like a bank account that gives you a maximum limit to the amount of money that can be deposited. Every day I had to decide which coins and notes to deposit to hit my maximum level. If a banknote was too large and couldn't be deposited, it was removed from the pile. If there were too many large banknotes and not enough coins I'd rebalance until I had a pile of cash to the value of 1,300 that I could bank.

Chocolate was a very large banknote. So were bread and pasta and cheese. Alcohol was a medium-sized one. Sugary things were high currency values too. But the great news was that salads, vegetables, tea, soup, and spices were like 5 pence pieces.

Once I knew what was what, I then recorded what I ate. Some days I ate more than 1,300. Other days I ate a bit less. EVERY day I recorded the score.

And guess what happened? Within eight weeks, I had hit my target weight, and I was able to run a 5k in around 25 minutes. I was fitter, lighter, healthier, and above all, pretty bloody pleased with myself for achieving my goal.

Why did I achieve it? Because I measured the results and inputs. I measured every day against the end-result and process/stage targets.

If I hadn't measured the calorie intake every day, I'd have fallen off the wagon, so to speak. I'd have told myself that 'one glass of wine won't hurt', and that 'I deserve a piece of chocolate today'. And, by the way, there is nothing wrong with either of those things. During my eight weeks, I had wine and chocolate, but I wrote them down and kept score. I knew that having those would mean having a little less of something else.

At the end of the day hitting your goals is about two things: 1) measuring and assessing your progress, and 2) mental toughness, of which more later.

Learn, Create, Develop, Earn, Burn

Goals can fit into any number of categories, but broadly orientate around three things:

1. To Have
2. To Do
3. To Be

A goal in the **'To Have'** category is about acquiring something as a possession. Your goal may be to have a Ferrari, the newest iPhone, your first home, the job you aspire to. It may be a simple and small thing, or something that's whopping and completely out of reach at the moment. Whatever the goal is, it's something you want to have.

A goal in the **'To Do'** category is one that you actually do. Not as in 'to buy the car you always wanted' (that's a *having* goal) but as in 'to run a marathon', or to take a trip around the world, to perform on stage at the Sydney Opera House, to bungee jump naked, to collect over £100,000 for charity, to bring up a child. It could be to do a favour, or just the ironing, cooking or gardening. It's something you are actively engaged in doing, and it is the doing of it that is your goal.

Lastly, there are goals about who or what you want **'To Be'**. You want to be slimmer, more muscular, a blonde, a doctor, a teacher, calmer, more reliable, more patient, free from a mortgage, a writer, a generous person, a loving person, the Prime Minister.

You can have as many goals as you like in any category, but my suggestion is you pick one or two from each category rather than have three from just one. Why? Because it's important to seek some balance. If all your goals are orientated towards having things, you deny yourself some opportunities to have fun and a sense of accomplishment actively doing something (Do), and you won't be working on improving yourself (Be). Conversely, if you only Do things you may end up with nothing material to show for all your efforts (Have), and you'll not evolve and develop (Be).

It's entirely up to you, but I have found that striking a balance feeds all areas of my desire to achieve, and I'm happier and better off for it.

Once you've decided on your goals, write down the process/stage steps to get there. What exactly are you going to need to get there, and what is the timescale you're going to set? Lastly, what's the budget you'll need to achieve them in both time and money.

Let's think about the money thing for a bit. If you want that Ferrari, you'll need to factor in saving £160,000 over a period of time working harder or smarter and earning more. If you have a goal to set up your own business, what's the seed capital you'll need and the ongoing operational financing until revenues and profitability start to put you in the black? To take the round the world trip you've dreamed of will need a budget. Even running a marathon is quite expensive, with shoes, supplements, running kit, race entries and more food because you're always hungry!

Make sure you have the spare cash available to undertake any of the goals you set yourself. Otherwise, you'll not get very far. It can help to set priorities between goals too.

I like to think of goals in terms of these five categories: CREATE, DEVELOP, LEARN, EARN, and BURN.

- I love to **CREATE** things - it just makes me feel alive. Whether it's a song or some writing, or creating sound from the piano, or creating solutions to problems. Creating is like spreading positive energy
- **DEVELOPING** is about evolving myself, ideas, relationships, projects
- **LEARNING** covers knowledge and skills. It's about developing an understanding of others, the environment and myself
- I want to **EARN** enough money to be comfortable and to have several earning streams so that I'm not wholly reliant on one. But it's more than about just money; it's about earning respect, earning the right to do things or be as I want to be
- **BURNING** is about energy. It's also about cash. Sometimes it's great to burn off the stress and tension of a day with a long run. Sometimes it's about burning cash and rewarding yourself or others.

Whatever categories work for you, just remember to keep a balance between Having, Doing and Being.

7. FORM HABITS, BREAK HABITS

Habits

According to research, habits account for approximately 40% of our daily behaviour. Four out of every ten things you do on any day are down to the habits that you have learned to adopt during your lifetime. None of us is born with habits. Sure, we have the instincts to eat, to keep safe, to sleep, to react in certain fundamental ways that ensure our survival at the most primitive level. But habits are different. These are things you habitually do or think or say that form almost half of who you are.

Ask people to think of a bad habit, and they might conjure up the image of someone smoking, or swearing, or picking their nose. But habits can also be useful. Taking the dog for a walk (exercise), doing your homework the day it's set rather than the last minute (never having things hanging over you), taking a morning run (exercise), visiting old parents (keeping them happy and healthy, doing your duty), talking to your boss each day on your drive home (keeping your boss happy and informed). There are so many good habits that many of us do.

How many bad habits do you have? List them down.

	My Bad Habits
1.	
2.	
3.	
4.	
5.	
6.	
7.	
8.	

Now list the good habits you have.

	My Good Habits
1.	
2.	
3.	
4.	
5.	
6.	
7.	
8.	

Next, ask your friends, family and colleagues what they think your good and bad habits are.

| | What my Colleagues and Friends say my Habits are ||
	Good	Bad
1.		
2.		
3.		
4.		
5.		
6.		
7.		
8.		

And finally, make a list of all the good habits you see in your friends, family and colleagues.

	Good Habits My Colleagues and Friends Have
1.	
2.	
3.	
4.	
5.	
6.	
7.	
8.	

(Top Tip: Don't list their bad habits and share with them unless they ask you to!!)

Do you want to stop some of your bad habits and adopt some new good ones? Me too. But it's hard. Really hard. Unless you deliberately focus on making the changes. And I bet you've already tried to start or stop some already. Anyone said on the 1st January that they'd quit drinking for a month? Or that it's now time to get fit, join a gym at huge costs only to barely use it after the first flush of enthusiasm has waned because it's hard, it's cold and dark after work, work's really busy actually, and there's a new series of Killing Eve (or something else) to watch instead? Have you tried giving up the biscuits when bored at work? Or said you'll stop wasting time online and start reading more?

I have. And I've failed more times than I've succeeded because it's hard.

"Will Power", people will say. "You just need stronger will power." As if there's something wrong with you because you didn't manage it. (These are the same people who also fail to break bad or form good habits most of the time!)

Let's go back to what we said in the first paragraph. Habits are formed. They are learned. It's a good job we do form them because I for one do not have nearly enough energy to think about 100% of what I do in a day. Having shorthands we do without thinking is brilliant. We just do them. No thought (or at least very little). So, good habits are very, very useful. On a kind of autopilot, we do just under half the things we do. But we also do the bad stuff.

Just as we learned the habits in the first place, we need to teach ourselves some new good ones to break and replace the bad ones.

Trying to break bad habits without replacing them with new good ones is almost impossible. Habits are rituals on autopilot requiring virtually no conscious thought. 'Will power' alone is the equivalent of an alcoholic going cold turkey. There's a conundrum. If I say don't think of an elephant, what do you have to do to think about not thinking about one? Get that image of an elephant out of your head. Now! Has it gone? That elephant? Are you sure the elephant isn't there anymore? Really?

Saying you're going to stop eating biscuits when bored through will power alone means you have to think about not eating biscuits. So, you're now thinking about biscuits. Biscuits are yum. But I can't have a biscuit as I said I wouldn't. But they taste so good. Those biscuits I'm not going to eat. My mouth is watering at the thought of the biscuits I'm not eating. Won't eat. I'm miserable now..... even more than I was before. I need a biscuit to cheer me up. One won't hurt. Just one. Not a lot of calories in one biscuit. Maybe two. I know it's not good to have one (or two), but I'll feel stronger tomorrow when I have a less stressful day. Honest.

(Tell me you're not thinking of having a biscuit right now!!)

What you need to do to break the habit is to replace it with another one. A more positive one. In this case, it could be to sip water every time you feel a bourbon cream craving. I don't know what the good habits are that you want to adopt but choose one and replace the bad one. A direct switch.

How long does a new habit take to form?

A study was undertaken at University College London and published in the European Journal of Psychology to determine how long it takes to form habits. Before this, the received wisdom was that it only took 21 days, based on localised observations of the time it took people to get used to losing a limb or gaining a new face, post operation.

In the study, 96 people were observed over a 12-week period. They all chose a new habit and recorded how their behaviour changed and whether it was automatic. The results varied from 18 days to a total of 254 days (extrapolating the data to project longer timelines). The average, however, was 66 days, or more than two months. While some people took less than the 21 days previously thought, the reality is that the length of time depends on the person, the circumstances and the behaviours they're seeking to change. Some habits are harder to form, just like some are harder to break. But, as a rule of thumb, you should assume that a new habit will take at least two months of conscious effort, repeating it again and again until it is an autopilot.

List the good habits you'll adopt to replace the bad ones.

	Good Habits I Will Adopt
1.	
2.	
3.	
4.	
5.	
6.	
7.	
8.	

Time Management and Prioritisation

Make excellent and effective Time Management a new habit. I'll wager that most people who have been on time management courses of one type or another don't really practise it. Why? Because none of us is in the habit of doing it. It's just too easy to carry on doing things the way we have always done them.

But I like checking my emails every few minutes - it makes me feel I'm not missing out on anything. And I want to stay in touch with everyone in the office, so they drop by my desk for a chat. I love it.

Old habits die hard. Let us, therefore, replace old and bad habits with some new ones. Replace them with the ones in the following sections.

If everything is a priority, then nothing is a priority. So many people have quotes attributed to them on a variation of that statement. It's true. If everything is important and is at the top of your priority list, then nothing is a priority over anything else. How would you determine what to start first? How would you rank them?

It's a fundamental skill to know how to prioritise, and this section deals with the best approach to doing just that. Use the Eisenhower method, and you'll never look at a task again in the same way. And more importantly, you'll never have a list of tasks that are all priority number one.

Eliminate the Non-Productive

If you're going to prioritise the things that are important to achieving your goal, then how about you also eliminate the non-productive things.

Write a list of the things that you do on a regular daily basis that are not geared towards achieving your goals. Not everything you do has to be so tunnel vision or obsessive about your performance acceleration program that you need to drive your family and friends mad with it all. You can still have (and should have) fun and relaxation. It's what makes us human and makes life interesting. But… there's a balance that needs to be struck.

If your goal is to accelerate your healthy-living performance, then you'd be better off getting active than sitting on the sofa eating Doritos playing space invaders. You'd be better off going for a walk or learning to dance, or having a Karaoke session for one and getting your blood pumping and energy flowing through your body. If your goal is to master an instrument, then you're going to have to limit the number of hours dedicated to EastEnders and Corrie. The Piano won't practise itself.

Some stuff is just not productive, so eliminate it.

Keep a diary of your activity for a week or two. Write down the things you do and how long they take. I had my team do a time and motion study at work once (they hated me for it). It was fascinating. The amount of contact time with clients was meagre. I mean really low, which isn't great for salespeople who live or die by their relationships and closeness to their customers. Early in my career, my old boss used to ask, "when was the last time you sold something to your desk or computer?" I started to spend more time with customers and less time in the office. Guess what happened? I began to sell a bit more. Then a lot more. And then even more. Why? Because I prioritised the customers, built relationships with them and knew what made them tick better than the salesperson from our competition.

The time and motion study showed up an issue. My team was spending a great deal of time doing stuff that wasn't productive. At all. We set about eliminating some of it, delegating other elements, and prioritising the stuff that needed to be done. That was at the end of June. For the second half of the year, we focused and prioritised. We consciously eliminated the things that added no value. Sales and customer satisfaction went up.

Win, win.

Write that list and keep that diary. In the next section, we'll look at the difference between Important and Urgent (and their opposites) and how you can categorise tasks to prioritise becoming a whole heap more effective.

Important vs Urgent

Dwight D. Eisenhower, the 34th President of the United States, once said, "I have two kinds of problems, the urgent and the important. The urgent are not important, and the important are never urgent". He was a truly great leader and military man, having been chief of staff of the army and Supreme Allied Commander in Europe. He knew something about making decisions, and important ones at that. The threat of the Soviets and the cold war drove him to sign and champion the bill that authorised the Interstate Highway Act in 1956. The belief was that when the Soviets struck, they would do so at the major cities meaning there was a need for a way to evacuate people quickly.

But is he entirely right? Are things ever exclusively important or urgent? They aren't in my world, and I hazard a guess they aren't in yours. I like to call our world….. the real world! Ever been told you need to complete an assignment by your boss at short notice a week before your annual performance review? I'd consider that assignment both important (if you don't do it it may impact your appraisal) and urgent (they need it by Wednesday for a presentation to the board). Because your boss didn't plan effectively, it became urgent for them, and they made it so for you. Sadly, the real world isn't quite as black and white as Eisenhower suggests. Now, if you're the boss and have the luxury of time, then you may have the ability to plan the important stuff effectively and never let it become urgent. But most of us aren't the ultimate boss. We all have lots of things pulling us in many directions in life. The competing demands of work, children, family, hobbies, football, mates, sleep, and social media. No matter how good you are at planning the important things, there will always be important things that are also urgent.

The house is burning down, and the safety of you and your loved ones is compromised. Pretty urgent and important to get them to safety I'd say. So, it's better to look at Eisenhower's statement from the perspective of all things being on a scale of both importance and urgency. Try it. Every time there is something you need to do, plot it based on its urgency and importance. That'll give you an obvious way to prioritise the myriad things you have to do in your life.

A search of the Internet will give you any number of important vs urgent matrices or worksheets. I guarantee you that applying this approach to everything will change your life. And, I mean everything - personal, family, work, etc.

What's the best way to categorise the tasks? Here's a simple four-box grid.

	Urgent	Not Urgent
Important	DO	PLAN
Unimportant	DELEGATE	ELIMINATE

Top Left - Important and Urgent

DO these first. DO them now. They are both important to you, and they are urgent, either because somebody else has imposed a deadline you have to comply with or because you've set the deadline yourself. Or, because they are a matter of life and death. There's no question that rescuing your family from a burning building is urgent and important....no-one set a deadline, but if you don't act urgently, dead is a possibility.

In your work life, a client may send you a request for something that means they will place an order for £1m of new business. That is urgent......DO it now. You may need to deliver your weekly sales forecast by 9 am on a Monday because your boss needs it for an unplanned review with the MD. No matter that you think that sucks because you have to give up some of the weekend to pull it together, it's both urgent and important. It's a real deadline with consequences if you don't deliver … you'll make your boss look bad, and that can only spell disaster for you. Perhaps the deadline for submission of a proposal to the Department of Education is approaching, and you have to write the executive summary before it's sent. You've got 3 hours to get it done. Your summary, which is likely to be read first but all reviewers, may make the difference between a lucrative contract for the supply of whiteboards to schools across the country, or not. That is urgent and important. DO it straight away.

You feel some chest pains while undertaking some DIY over the weekend. The bookcase you're building for your daughter may be important, but suddenly your own health concerns are urgent. Stop whatever you're doing that's important but not urgent and focus on the urgent and important signs that something might not be right with your health and get down to the hospital.

You get the picture. If it's urgent AND important, DO it first.

Note: If someone else is better placed to do it for you can move an item to bottom left as long as you know that it will get done on time and to the standard you need it to be.

Top Right - Important but Not Urgent

This is where you should live. In box two, at the top-right position. Most of your time should be here, on the goals you have that are really important to moving things forward. If you spend most of your time here, then very few of the goals you have should land in the top left 'urgent' pile. If you can master focusing your time on the bigger goals – the ones that need planning and execution over the longer term – then you'll find that you are both a time management ninja (oh yeah!) and you're leaping ahead quickly.

This box is all about PLANNING. Create your goal and PLAN for success. It's not urgent, so you don't need to fight fires on it. You have the luxury of a bit of time to think about what you need to do and by when to make it happen.

What kind of things should go in this quadrant? If your goal is to lose weight and get fit, it'll go in here. Why? Because it's going to take some planning and time. A crash diet a week before your wedding isn't going to work. You'll make yourself ill, and the champagne will go to your head too quickly so the photos may be remembered for all the wrong reasons. Planning for it, just like you would for the dress, the flowers, the venue, the rings etc. is the best plan of action. And getting fit doesn't take a short period of time. I recently needed to get fitter for skiing … I'd been unwell a few times earlier in the year so had to stop running and rowing training. I had about two weeks to 'get fit'. I tried, but there just wasn't enough time to train the right muscles (which I didn't know I even had) or to increase my oxygen levels sufficiently.

Consequently, I was a bit sluggish and got out of breath too quickly. Now, in my case, illness meant I couldn't implement my plan effectively, so I'm not going to be too hard on myself. If I had the opportunity to do so, I would have got a bit fitter, done more squats and prepared better. By the end of the week at altitude, I was feeling great, and, the best bit of all, I broke no bones and tore no muscles.

Your goal for writing the next Pulitzer prize-winning novel goes in this box. If you want to get a promotion to the next level up at work, it goes here. If you're studying for your PhD, you guessed it, it's in the PLANNING quadrant. A' Levels, MBA, wedding, holiday planning, house buying, children making, family gatherings, parties, climbing mount Everest, sailing around Britain, composing a smash hit that'll knock Ed Sheeran out of the charts, career planning ... they are all in this box.

Bottom Left - Unimportant but Urgent

This box is all about DELEGATION. For many people, delegation doesn't come naturally. The idea that things which you are perfectly capable of doing should be passed off to someone else doesn't sit well with a lot of people, especially if you're quite action-oriented.

Do you like cleaning your house? Really? Weird! Even if you do, is it worth your time and effort? Could you do something of higher value while someone else cleans? If cleaning your house would take you four hours a week and you pay a cleaner £10 per hour, could you spend those four hours making £20 per hour? Or could you spend that time working on the items in your to-do list that drive your performance forward? Even if you don't make money during that time, achieving something of higher value than £40 is an investment in your future.

Tax return time! Did your heart just sink? Get your accountant to do it. Yes, it'll cost you, but they may be able to save you some tax, and you can finish your dissertation, music practice, book, business plan, presentation for the promotion at work, etc., while they do what they are trained to do.

One thing about this quadrant - though it says the tasks are unimportant, it may be that they are reasonably important, but they are things you are either not capable of doing or aren't particularly good at. Things can go in this box if it would be better for someone else to do them so that your time is free to focus on the important tasks in the matrix. It is important to pay the school fee cheque, but you may want to delegate the administration of it to your spouse. Or it may be important to clean out the guinea pig hutch, but you can delegate that to your 16-year-old in return for a bit of extra pocket money.

Bottom line - whether the task is unimportant or not, it's about DELEGATION in this box. Let someone else take the strain so you can focus on those things that move your goals forward.

Bottom Right - Unimportant and Not Urgent

Can you think of the things you do in the day that are neither urgent nor important? There will probably be quite a few. Right in the middle of doing something important your mind wanders and your thumb presses on Facebook to check what your friends are up to. Quite amusing I'm sure to see the picture of someone's lunch at some fancy restaurant, or someone who is only a 'Facebook friend' who you'd never actually socialise with in real life bragging about how their middle child has won the school prize for badminton. Oh, and the angry campaigner who posts everything they can about what an arse Donald Trump is. It's all really quite fun. But was it urgent that you check FB? I mean, did you do it because if you hadn't something terrible would have happened? Or was it important for you to know about Millie's badminton prowess, or that the butternut squash risotto was to die for?

There are a time and place for checking your buddy's latest Trump rant, and that's when you are relaxing, or when everything else is completed in the three other quadrants. I use FB status checking as an example, but there will be loads of others. That chat, browsing for something you don't need, replying to an email (quite a lot of emails generally fall in this category), checking the football or cricket scores, basically, all those procrastination activities that just aren't important or urgent.

Now, lest I be accused of being a dinosaur about social media (I've been called so much worse!) it's not that I have a thing against social media in general, but it can be (mostly is) a massive time waster if you're looking to achieve lots and accelerate your performance. Read my other book, '60 Ways to Hurray!' and you'll learn that my favourite time to check social media is while sitting on the loo!

If something cannot be categorised as either urgent or important, then it goes in the bottom right box.

If something is in the bottom right box, then your job is to ELIMINATE it. Simply do not do it. Get rid of it. Bin it. Forget about it. Don't waste time on it. Nuke it.

Note: Many things that fall in this category may be habits, and habits are tough to break as we've seen in a previous section. You need to replace them with good habits to truly make a lasting change.

80/20 Rule

In 1896 an Italian engineer and economist published a paper at the University of Lausanne in which he showed that approximately 80% of the land in Italy was owned by 20% of the population. Joseph M. Juran, an American engineer and management consultant, suggested that this ratio of 80/20 might be applicable in many other settings.

If you want chapter and verse on the Pareto Principle, then grab yourself a copy of "The 80/20 Principle" by Richard Koch. It's fascinating.

In business, have you ever noticed that most of your company's revenue comes from only a small handful of the largest clients? Do the analysis, and I bet it'll show you the principle in action.

When Pareto discovered that 80% of the land was distributed amongst 20% of the population, he set about looking at other countries and found a similar distribution.

What about income? Yes, that too. Approximately 20% of the wealthiest people in the world take about 80% of the available income.

The principle can be seen at work in sports. It can be seen in science and software development, hazards and injuries, maths and plenty of other applications.

On the basis that it appears to be a universal truth, it stands to reason that 80% of the results you obtain will come from 20% of the inputs. In other words, 20% of everything you do contributes towards you achieving 80% of your success. The other 80% of your efforts deliver only the last 20%.

Think about that for a minute......4/5ths of all that you do is not contributing very much at all. In a 5-day working week, it's the equivalent of Monday's work enabling you to achieve £800 of your £1,000 sales target, while Tuesday, Wednesday, Thursday and Friday together only produce £200!!

What are the activities that generate the results you want if you're setting up your own business? It'll be a combination of things such as prospecting, talking to clients, setting up the company website, filing various forms with companies' house, etc. At different stages of the process, different things become more important, and it becomes clear what is delivering your results.

How do you identify what the 20% of activities are that make the difference and enable you to hit the 80%? That's not so easy, unfortunately.

Make a list of what you're doing and attribute a value to it depending on how much of an impact it has on achieving the results you need. If making a client call yields a strong lead for your business, give that a 1. If searching for pictures of blue unicorns on google doesn't get you to where you want to be, give it a 5. Over time you'll see what the 20% of activities are that truly make a difference. You can then choose to spend more time doing them.

Focus on the things that make the most significant impact. Spend your time there. Then do the rest or get someone else to do them. Remember to apply Eisenhower's grid.

What's with the Tomato?

Back in the 1980s, it was quite novel to have a kitchen timer in the shape of a tomato.

What has a tomato-shaped timer got to do with anything? The Italian for tomato is Pomodoro, and an Italian-born man named Francesco Cirillo invented something called the Pomodoro Technique.

The technique uses the kitchen timer to chunk up the amount of time spent on tasks before a break is taken. The idea is that if you are interrupted continuously while undertaking an important job, it will take longer and be of lower quality. Set aside some undivided time for each task. Complete the task and have a short break.

Sounds simple…not the kind of thing that needs a whole technique, surely! The thing is, we are all brilliant at getting distracted. Ping…oh, a text. Ring…hello Janet, of course, I can help……mmmm must check social media……Eva's latest story of her online dating conquest from the weekend is so much more interesting than my work…..

Get the picture?

- You first need to decide on the task to be completed…use your Eisenhower list
- Then you set the timer (tomato-shaped or not) for 25 minutes and work on it uninterrupted until the timer goes off
- Now have a rest for 3-5 minutes
- Set the timer again for 25 minutes and crack on uninterrupted
- Time for another short break
- And repeat
- After every four 25-minute sessions give yourself a longer break for 15-30 minutes
- Then back to the beginning
- Rinse and repeat

What kind of tasks would you devote the chunks of time to? Anything, as long as they are in Eisenhower's boxes 1 and 2 and are things that are in the 20% that get results.

But what about emails? I hear you ask. It's not possible to devote all your time to actions that move the needle. If you get 250 emails a day, you have to read them, and other things need doing too. Well, rather than check your emails while you're working on something important, turn off those interrupting alerts and leave them alone. Then, make emails one of the tasks you schedule for one (or more) of the 25-minute sessions. Once time is up, move on to something else and leave emails until another session.

That's called batching and will help make life simpler. Only check emails at specific times of day, when you've scheduled to do so. Make them just another task, so they don't invade your important and game-changing actions.

No one ever wishes they spent more time on emails......so make a pact with yourself to spend less. Just batch them three times a day. Schedule them in and listen to the Pomodoro.

Manage Your Energy

How many of you have a job contract that specifies your working hours? 08:30- 17:30 with a one-hour break for lunch, maybe? How many of you have to be in an office or shop or another workplace, physically present between certain hours? And do you find that the prescribed hours are sometimes (or often) just not enough? I'll bet you put more hours in and work harder regularly.

It's a pretty common story, particularly for those running their own businesses, in client-facing roles or middle to senior management. The list of things that needs to get done is so long that you work a few extra hours to break the back of it. You feel good about getting on top of everything. Your boss is happy and sees your ability to cope well with pressure, and extra work so gives you a little more responsibility. Your list grows a little longer, so you decide to put in a few more hours, maybe over the weekend. Fast forward a few years, and you are regularly clocking up 12-14-hour days. You're tired most of the time, yet you don't sleep properly. You're not connecting with your family very well when not working because you're exhausted. You're not eating properly because you don't have time and as for exercise, well that's something you only get when you walk to the sandwich shop and back before sitting at your desk.

One day you realise you're exhausted. You start to blame the job. You become dissatisfied and begin looking for something else, where you can get a better 'work-life' balance. If you're unlucky, you may get ill as a result of this overwork. Then you find something new and with the best of intentions tell yourself that this time will be different; this time you'll manage your time better and have the work-life balance you promised your family and yourself. But, history has a habit of repeating itself, over and over and over again.

Is managing time the best way to manage your workload? Is working extended hours the answer? A study published in the Harvard Business Review suggests it may be ultimately the wrong way to become more productive.

Schwartz, president and founder of the Energy Project in New York City, and McCarthy, its senior vice president, embarked on a study at Wachovia Bank to see whether managing energy is a better way than managing time. They took over 100 employees from 12 of its regional banks and put them through a course consisting of four modules, each focusing on one aspect of the four dimensions of energy. Then they measured the revenue for three different types of loans and compared it to several control groups who had not been on the courses.

The energy study group showed a year-on-year increase in revenues 13% higher than the control groups. Revenue from deposits was up 20%. 68% of the participants said there had been a positive impact on relationships with customers. 71% said there had been a noticeable impact on their own productivity and performance.

Those statistics are staggeringly good. More than double-digit revenue growth. Deposits up by a fifth. Seven out of 10 participants claiming to have better productivity and relationships with customers. All from managing their energy better.

What are the four types of energy to focus on?

1. Physical
2. Emotional
3. Mental
4. Spiritual

1. **Physical Energy - Giving the body what it needs**

You need enough physical energy to be able to perform. At the most fundamental level you need food and sleep, but what about the quality of the nutrition or the duration and quality of your sleep? It's not just about these two, however. There is also exercise and rest.

At the start of the study, participants were asked a series of questions about all four facets of energy and were scored to show whether they were heading for an energy crisis. The questions asked about physical energy were around whether a participant sleeps seven to eight hours a night, whether they skip breakfast or simply eat something that's not nutritious, whether they work out enough and if they take breaks during the day.

They then set about changing any poor habits, including things like scheduling a time to go to bed, eating smaller amounts of more nutritious foods more often during the day, taking breaks every 90-120 minutes to coincide with the ultradian rhythms (even taking a 20-minute walk to get exercise). And they ensured they took time to exercise at least three times a week.

2. <u>Emotional Energy - Quality</u>

Energy can be constructive or destructive. Think of the wind. Its energy can be incredibly constructive, powering wind farms, enabling the ships on the first trade routes to bring spices and other fine goods from the East, it can blow the smog that sits over cities away so they can breathe again. And yet it can also be the most destructive force. Just think of hurricane Sandy.

Unlike the wind, we have a choice about how we channel our energy. We can choose what the quality is. We've all felt strong emotions before; love, anger, fear, resentment, irritation, and so on. But have you ever stopped to think about the fact that you can control them? I know I've sometimes been in a bad mood and felt like staying in a bad mood because I was pretty ticked off with something. I felt like wallowing. If I become irritated by someone, it's not that they are necessarily irritating. It is my issue, not theirs. It's my reaction to them which I can take control of.

If we can take control of our emotions, it stands to reason we can improve the quality of our energy. But that requires us to become aware of how we're feeling at various points in the day and put in place strategies to help manage our emotional reserves.

One way to reduce or remove the fight or flight response of stress is to take deep breaths - deep abdominal breathing where you exhale for five to six seconds. Not only are you buying time before reacting, but you are inducing relaxation and recovery.

A way to top up your emotional energy is to express appreciation to others. Not only does it make the receiver feel great, but it has a powerful impact on energy levels and feeling of wellbeing. Spend time recognising people publicly or privately. Send them an email, or better still a more personal hand-written note. Mentoring and coaching others can aid this too; identifying the good things they are doing and helping them continue to learn and grow. Make sure you give enough time to this critical energiser, the by-product of which is an increase in loyalty and team spirit.

3. <u>Mental Energy - Focus</u>

Do you consider yourself to be a multi-tasking hero? Can you focus on a conference call, IM someone and read and respond to your emails all at the same time? If you can, that's great. But if you do it regularly, then go to the bottom of the class. You may get a sense of achievement, a macho feeling that you're on top of your game, or you may feel that you have to otherwise you'll never cope with the volume of stuff going on. But what you're really doing is short-changing everyone you're interacting with and setting yourself up for fatigue.

I don't know if you've ever checked your own efficiency in doing tasks. It won't surprise you to learn that I have. I do it quite regularly because there are so many things I'm trying to achieve all at the same time. If I set out to write a chapter of a book, it usually takes me around two hours for the first draft. The days when I do this at 06:30 and focus purely on the writing, I get it nailed in one go, and on time. If I attempt to write at the weekend when there are chores to do, fun things with family or calls from friends, it takes me way longer. The total elapsed time may be six hours because I've been doing those other things too. During those hours I've done a bit of writing, then answered a call, a little more writing, then done a chore, then a family activity, then some more writing. But if I add up the total amount of time writing it comes to approximately 2hours 30mins to 2hours 45mins. I have taken between 25-37.5% longer to complete the same task because every time I sit back down to start writing again there's a little inertia to get over and I'm no longer in the zone. I have to remind myself where I was and what I was trying to convey. Every time you flit from one thing to another, you are subjecting yourself to 'switching time', making you at least 25% less efficient and fatiguing your poor brain. If you could change your working practices, you could achieve the same amount of work and do it in 8 hours instead of 10…that's 2 hours you can have back for yourself and the things you want to do, every day!

We work in cycles for between 90-120 minutes. If there's a task that requires focus and concentration, then get up from your desk and go into another room. Turn off your phone and close your email and IM applications. Then focus until you're finished (or you need a break as above in Physical Energy). Only once you are done, switch everything back on.

The most efficient and least mentally fatiguing way to work is to batch tasks and concentrate on completing the batch before moving on. Don't answer email all the time, schedule it two or three times a day and clear it. The same goes for other things; batch your learning tasks, expenses, business planning, accounting, writing, tuba practice, gardening.

Schedule time in your calendar for the most important tasks each day and do them as the first tasks, before you open email or attend to other things. This way you'll get to 10 am and feel you've already had a productive day, even before the noise of the day begins. The key to this is to decide the night before what the most important task is and then put it in your calendar to make sure everyone else knows you're busy and so that, more importantly, *you* know that you're busy with an activity which will make a long-term positive impact on your goals.

4. <u>Spiritual Energy - Human Spirit</u>

If you have you ever been in a situation where you've had to do something that does not sit well with your values, you'll know how energy-draining it can be. We've seen earlier that people want to be consistent with their beliefs, values and goals, so managing or improving spiritual energy means needing to focus on the meaning and values we attribute to ourselves and our job or goal.

Establishing rituals will aid your spirit in these:

1. Doing what you do best and enjoy most (remember that if you enjoy it and want to do it, it's not going to feel like 'work.'

2. Allocating enough time and energy to the important areas of your life (that work-life balance thing is necessary to stimulate an increase in performance)
3. Living your core values daily

Many people say their family is the most important thing to them and yet they don't devote as much time to them as they could. Whatever you consider to be the most important aspects of your life, devote enough energy to each. Establishing specific rules and rituals will help. Turning the phone off at mealtimes, or on date night, or playing the guitar to your son's drumming...whatever it is, do it regularly.

I once worked at a financial institution in a tower block in London. The view was amazing, and far below, I could see people busily moving along Oxford Street and Tottenham Court Road as they went about their mornings. My boss asked me if I could shoot one of them from up here (I'm not kidding, and he wasn't joking). I asked what he meant. He said that they were so small and faceless that it'd be easy to get a high-powered rifle and shoot one. I resigned shortly afterwards. People are the most important part of my life - the value I put on interacting with others, helping them, laughing with them, engaging with them is one of my most important drivers. His attitude was prevalent across the sales floor - people were just walking opportunities to make lots of cash. I resigned, and he called me some very fruity names. I got out and found something else that fitted with my core values. (They went bust, by the way!)

I've read about batching, managing energy, not multi-tasking, and getting a better work-life balance a few times in the past and I've always thought "yeah right like that's even possible in the modern working world". We seem to be expected to be on email 24/7, even when on holiday. Our bosses and teams expect instant responses. And our workloads are so big that we have to multitask just to cope.

I can tell you from my own experiments and experience that it is possible to do all of the things suggested in this chapter. More than that, Schwartz and McCarthy's study suggests that if you want to improve performance, you'd better start putting some new working practices and rituals in place to accelerate towards your goals and towards being a more energetic individual, for your work, your family and friends, and for yourself.

Can't Do Everything

You own your goals. You can put them in the Eisenhower matrix and decide where they go. But what if others want your time? It's not really a what if…just as you want the time of others to help you, they will want your input too.

I've read many books that espouse being ruthless with the allocation of your time. They tell you to focus on your own goals and let others find another way to achieve what they want without distracting you. I agree with it to a point - we all need to be clear on what we're trying to achieve and how much time and effort that's going to take.

We are part of society, and society only works if there's some give and take. Have you any friends or colleagues who are all take, take, take? You help them and they never really return any favours? Some don't even thank you? I have. And I've sought to eliminate them –the energy sappers.

As part of society, we all need to contribute actively. What you put in, you get out. Remember from the section on Influence and Persuasion that if we do good things for others, they are more inclined to reciprocate. So being part of other people's bottom left, Delegation, box is a good thing. Hopefully, you will do things for others because they are important to you, and their success is also.

But there is a skill in saying 'NO'. You can't do everything. You need to sleep, to do your work, spend time with your family, work on your goals. Your time is limited, and you need to marshal it well; otherwise, you won't be able to get as much done as you want.

Saying 'No' comes naturally to some but not to others. I naturally want to try and help others so can get distracted easily, especially as by helping someone else I get a bit of a kick –a feel-good moment – as well as being distracted from the more difficult but important task I'm in the middle of. Helping others can be a brilliant form of procrastination, so I work hard to minimise these distractions.

If you do say no to someone, be polite and respectful. One day you'll need something from them. Give them a reason and stick to it - scheduling conflict, an important project taking all your time right now, can't as on a call, picking up Daisy from Ballet at that time, not something you feel comfortable with, etc.

Sometimes people will ask for help via email. If they send to a few people and you're just one of them, you could take it that someone else will answer, so you can ignore it.

It may be impossible to ignore the request, in which case try to help. There are ways of helping that don't necessarily mean spending hours doing the task for them. One tactic is to redirect it back to the requester – e.g. *"Have you checked the information on the intranet under funding options?" "Did you go to SharePoint to look at the termination rights in the contract?" "Have you checked with Dave what the latest statistics are?"*

Or delegate to someone who is better equipped to help them.

According to Steve Jobs, focus is about saying "NO". Train yourself to say no to tasks or requests that de-focus you from your own goals. After all, you're only human and cannot possibly do everything.

Delegating Effectively

What can you do to get more done? Delegate. We've talked about that in the section on Important vs Urgent actions. But how do you best utilise the power of your network to help you achieve more?

Here are seven steps to delegation heaven:

1. **What do you want to delegate?** Use the Important vs Urgent matrix from earlier. Those things that are urgent but not important are ripe for delegation, but anything can be delegated if there is someone capable of doing the task.

2. **Who do you know who's best placed to help?** One of your network? Who might have the time or can provide the guidance you need? Is there someone who'd like to earn a bit of extra money who has the skills to make a good job of it? Or can you get a virtual assistant to help? I've used an offshore virtual assis-

tant on projects before, and it was very cost-effective and straight forward. Plus, it was quick.

3. **Be crystal clear about what is needed**, in what format, by when, in how much detail, etc. The clearer you are the less room there is for misunderstanding and the better quality the result will be. You don't need to be prescriptive about how they do it, just about what the expected outcome is. I'd recommend not being prescriptive with the how. They aren't you, and everyone has different ways of getting things done. Just because you do it a particular way doesn't mean they should have to.

4. **Explain the why.** You've learned about creating a purpose for everything you do and how anchoring to the 'Why' helps the What and How be delivered. Provide a really clear context to the person helping you. If they understand why it's important and what the purpose of the overall task is, then they are more likely to do a good job.

5. **Are there any files, tools, articles or other documents they'll need to do the job?** Make sure they have these and know how to use them. There's no point delegating something unless the person has the resources available to do it effectively.

6. **Get them to own the whole task.** If they own it end-to-end, they are more likely to want to do a good job. If you only delegate some of the tasks, you're setting yourself up for confusion and lack of ownership with someone who probably won't have as much invested in getting it right or completed on time.

7. **What are the expected outcomes, deliverables and timescales?** Be clear about these and get the person

who's helping to confirm back what they have understood. Don't just ask them if they've understood you. It's a closed question which doesn't test understanding. Ask them to repeat back to you what needs doing, by when and in what format.

Once the task is completed satisfactorily, remind them of the **'why'** and how this has helped. If you engaged their services professionally (e.g. a virtual assistant), then leave good feedback or a testimonial. If someone has done you a favour, then give them a gift. And no matter whether they did it for free or a fee heap praise and thanks on them. Remember this was a task you'd have had to have done were it not for them.

The Importance of Exercise

A bottle of red wine's worth of blood every minute. That's 750ml of blood every sixty seconds coursing through the 100,000 miles of blood vessels in your brain, feeding it with oxygen, energy and hormones. The brain receives 20% of the blood and oxygen produced, and weighs in at 3lb in weight, 2lb of which is fat!

If you deprive your brain of oxygen for more than 5-6 minutes, you'll die. The 100 billion neurones will cease firing, and there will be no remaining evidence that there was ever a life lived. It'll just be a lump of fat.

The neurones of a foetus in the early stages of development grow at 250,000 per minute, enabling it to function and grow before birth. As a baby, toddler and child, brain development is rapid with new skills such as walking, talking, motor coordination, communication, playing, squabbling, tantrum-throwing and how to cry to get what you want being learned. Then school follows where knowledge is acquired, followed by experience ·gained, jobs, marriage, children and, at last, retirement. Along this journey, memories are being laid down, and a unique map of the world produced that combines nature, nurture and experience.

As we get older, our ability to learn new things fades or can take us considerably longer to master them. Our memories can wain and can start to lose some cognitive function through degenerative conditions.

But the good news is that you can help yourself as you age by looking after your brain through nothing more sophisticated than exercise. In studies undertaken by Dr Wendy A. Suzuki – Professor of Neural Science and Psychology in the Centre for Neural Science at New York University – she shows how aerobic exercise is the single most significant contributor to improving our brain function and memory.

Her research shows that the Hippocampus, or the area of the brain where memories are formed and stored, grows when regular exercise is taken. New brain cells are created, increasing our capacity to learn, remember and understand things.

Dr Suzuki found, relatively unsurprisingly, that there are short term benefits of exercising. One workout will increase the amount of dopamine, noradrenaline and serotonin in the brain, improving mood and ability to focus and shift attention. This change lasts only about two hours after a single workout, but for those two hours, you are an improved version of yourself, even having better reaction times for a while.

It's when exercise is undertaken regularly – long term – that permanent changes happen. The hippocampus increases in size, the physiology and function changes with higher attention function dependent on the prefrontal cortex. Mood changes last longer. Regularly increased levels of neurotransmitters improve cognitive function and memory.

But the best bit of all is the effect exercise has on protecting the brain from neurodegenerative diseases and decline in older age. If you want to be strong in later life, you need to build muscle. If you're going to ward off brain, cognitive or memory degeneration then you need the biggest and best hippocampus and prefrontal cortex you can get. You can get those by exercising over your lifetime.

Everybody has heard that exercise is good for them and that they'll concentrate better, sleep better, and make better decisions, faster if done regularly. It will keep you in shape, and you'll feel much better than if you don't. Those hormones and neurotransmitters will rush through your brain's 100,000 miles of blood vessels telling you that you're good.

A few of the positive impacts that come from exercise are:

Learning - There's a protein called 'brain-derived neurotrophic factor' which invites neutron growth. It can help prevent brain cells from eroding, make them work better, helps deal with stress and generally provides the best environment for brains to function and develop. Guess what? Exercise makes neutrons fire, and when neutrons fire, this protein is released, and when this protein is released, brain cells work better. In turn, this means that our ability to learn is enhanced.

Memory - The process of creating new neurons is called neurogenesis, and in rodents, it's been shown that exercise doubled the rate of neurogenesis in the hippocampus. It also increases the length of the neurons and the number of dendrite spines. These factors have been shown to improve hippocampus function and were measured using memory tests. A study of runners from 2016 showed significantly higher connectivity between parts of their brains as compared to a group of non-runners. The greater connectivity was in areas that control decision making, multi-tasking, memory and attention. So, get running (or walking, or cross-fit, or rowing, cycling, swimming). Whatever you do, just do it and make it a habit.

Concentration and Attention - For a long time, exercise has been known to ease the symptoms of ADHD in children and adults due to the neurotransmitter, dopamine, being dumped into the brain, calming the mind.

Creativity - If I could give you a recipe to be 81% more creative, would you take it? Yet again, it is exercise that has been proven to be the best way to get that boost. In 2014 a study took 176 people, dividing them into a group of walkers and non-walkers (sedentary). They were asked to complete a creativity test, either while walking (group 1) or sitting (group 2). Those who were exercising at the time of taking the test scored 81% higher than the control group. The next time you're looking for creativity.

Mental Health - Dr Jon Ratey is associate clinical professor of psychiatry at Harvard Medical School and has written a book called "Spark: The Revolutionary New Science of Exercise and the Brain". He talks of exercise as being like taking Prozac and Ritalin because they, like exercise, increase the amount of dopamine, norepinephrine and serotonin in the brain. Through exercise, the brain can balance hormones and help alleviate depression, protecting us (to a degree) from stress. The brain uses more glucose when exercising, and in a 2016 study, they found that it created more neurotransmitters, which can aid in tempering depression.

If you want to perform at your best AND protect your brain for the future, then you'd be well advised to exercise regularly. It doesn't need to be marathon running. It doesn't need to be particularly strenuous. But it does need to be regular and to elevate your heart rate. Three sessions of 30 minutes a week is all it takes and is undoubtedly an investment of time worth making for such amazing benefits.

8. MENTAL TOUGHNESS

Discipline

There is no doubt that to push yourself to achieve something you're going to need discipline. It's really easy to *want* to get fit, change job, write a book, get grade 8 French Horn. But while running the movie in your mind so you can see the eventual outcome is a worthwhile thing to do it isn't going to get your waist down from 38 inches to 34. It won't, of itself, enable you to show your friends and family the finished book. If you only visualise your French Horn recital at the Festival Hall, your audience will demand their money back quicker than they can say 'Stockhausen'.

Visualising is critical, and I urge you to do it, often. Seeing the end result, feeling what to feels like to have completed it, hearing your loved ones congratulate you - these all help with your motivation. Debra Searle, in her solo rowing quest across the Atlantic, played the movie in her mind so she could see what crossing the finish line would be like. Had she not done that it's more than likely she'd have ended up just like the other single rowing teams who didn't finish at all.

But did the movie make her row every day? Not entirely. It will have helped motivate her, but the fact is that rowing is incredibly boring. If you've ever sat on a Concept 2 in the gym and set about doing a 30-minute session, I'm sure, like me, after 5 minutes you're wondering if it's too soon to stop yet. Debra had to do it every day for 111 days. That required discipline.

The received wisdom is that self-discipline is a measure of will-power. The idea goes that you can be self-disciplined for a certain amount of time, but once you've used up your will power chips for the day then discipline fades faster than the orange glow from a tanning salon session.

Scientists used to believe that will power fatigued the brain and that the demise of self-discipline was because blood sugar dropped. This is called the Energy Model. Daniel Molden of North Western University wasn't satisfied with this explanation. Very little evidence existed, so he set about looking at levels of self-discipline and glucose.

He took a group of people who had fasted and were well-rested before undertaking the tasks. One half undertook a mentally challenging task. The other half undertook a task requiring minimal mental exertion. Consistent with the energy theory, he found that the group who had done the mentally challenging job dropped off when undertaking a second one. However, when he measured the blood glucose level after the exertion and compared it to the level taken before, there was no difference. Mental exertion does not, in fact, deplete blood glucose after all.

The Energy Model also posits that if you increase blood glucose levels, the person will have a greater capacity to exert more will power and hence be more self-disciplined. He tested this after the first mentally exerting task by asking part of the group to rinse their mouths with a sugar solution, but not swallow it. Another part of the group rinsed with an artificial sweetener and again did not swallow it. They were then both asked to complete another mentally taxing task. The group that had rinsed with artificial sweetener showed no improvement, but the group that had rinsed with a sugar solution showed a greater level of will power again.

That is very interesting. Mental exertion was shown not to deplete blood glucose and to rinse with, but not swallow a sugary solution was shown not to increase glucose levels either. So why the increased will power after rinsing with sugar?

The answer is that the brain registers that a carbohydrate is in the mouth and perceives a reward coming; after all, the brain craves the sugar hit it gets from carbohydrates. This has the effect of increasing motivation to succeed in the mentally taxing task. Will power improves, and thus, self-discipline.

So, what's the lesson here? If your concentration is waning, or your motivation to continue doing the task at hand is lacking, or you've already exerted yourself quite a bit, rinse your mouth out with a sugary syrup.

You're going to want to swallow it. It tastes great, and your brain craves it. Tempting as it might be to swallow, you need to go all counterintuitive. Don't swallow it.

Unemotional

I would describe myself as an emotional person. I did, after all, shed a tear when Scott married Charlene on the Australian soap opera 'Neighbours'. It was first broadcast in the UK on the 8th November 1988 and, living only a 3-minute walk away from school, my best mates, and I went back to mine and watched it during our lunch break. 'Suddenly' by Angry Anderson played as the ceremony took place and I shed a tear. It was beautiful.

'Varcoe! You wuss.' They all hurled at me, shattering the perfection of the union between Jason Donovan's horrendous mullet and Kylie's flowing permed locks.

They knew I was a softie, but they knew I could get a bit punchy too. Like the time one of the older boys tried to pick a fight with my younger, rugby-playing sized, brother. He could most definitely handle himself against the equally stocky 1st XV team member. This chap could eat the likes of my lanky, slender frame for breakfast.

My little brother was getting a bit of heat, so I leapt to his defence. The volley of words, for words were all I had over this lump, came out with the ferocity of an erupting volcano, causing everyone in the way to step back in disbelief. The bulldog's attention moved from my brother to me. Seizing his opportunity for a guaranteed win, he pushed me back against the wall. The collective gasp of the paused faces floated above and around us.

I got a pasting as a reward for losing some self-control. My brother wasn't too impressed, either.

Emotions can strike us at any time for any reason, and while it is OK to whimper at a film or get all self-righteous sometimes, it's much better for the career, long term relationships and achieving one's goals to keep the emotions in check. There are a time and a place for strong emotions, and the workplace isn't generally one of them.

1. Recognise and acknowledge emotions

In the section 'Emotional vs Logical' we saw that it's not a good idea to ignore the Chimp. It's big, stronger than our logical selves, and pretty volatile. The emotions are there, whether you like them or not. The first thing to do when managing emotions is to recognise them.

When you feel nervous, upset, angry, worried, irritated, bored, or excited, take a moment to recognise what you're feeling. Then think about why you're reacting in this way. What is it about the situation that makes you feel like that? Is it justifiable? How are others reacting to it? Is your reaction in proportion or comparable?

2. Ensure that feelings and emotions can be shared

I had a boss once who delighted in telling us that 'A problem shared is not a problem halved. A problem shared is a problem shelved.' He meant it in the context of some action needing to be taken......tell someone else about it and get them to do it. Hey presto, it is shelved for you, and it gets done! Result. He was an arch delegator.

It is very cathartic to express feelings to someone who you trust to listen in a non-judgemental way. Find yourself a coach or mentor and talk through your emotions with them. In expressing your feelings, there is a release from the pent-up emotional state, something that can be quite damaging if not addressed. If you talk, someone may have good advice or experience that will help you deal with the emotion appropriately.

3. If the emotion becomes too much, walk away

There are times when emotions run high and are too much to bear. If you've ever experienced grief, you'll know that a tidal wave of emotion can envelop you, rendering you useless for a time. That is part of the grief process. It's natural and good. At times like that the best approach is to withdraw and let it pass.

So too with anger or frustration. I remember a meeting I was in with a chap whose nickname at work was 'the riddler'. If you wanted to know what features the product he was responsible for had that dealt with X or Y, he'd start by telling you about Z and then how it didn't have G, but if you did something it could have X but probably not Y, unless you stumbled on P. It was exhausting! And frustrating. Everything took three times longer because I had to clarify what he meant every few sentences. The frustration was palpable. The irritation felt like boiling over. I had to walk away from meetings with him many times for fear of voicing my frustration and anger in a way that neither of us would have easily come back from.

4. Harness the power of positive emotions

Positive people are energy givers. They radiate electricity. Seemingly nothing is too much trouble. They manage to look at the positives in difficult situations. This is the one emotion you want in your business, project, team, or on your own. The more positive the vibes, the easier things will seem and the less stressed you, and the rest of the group, will be.

Harness this emotion and use it to your advantage. Make sure you have a positive mindset amongst the team before a project starts, as well as during it. Allow the positivity to feed other ideas.

Have fun, share positivity and include everyone in this magical emotion.

5. Do what's right

You know that feeling when you're torn between what your head and heart are telling you. Do you go with your heart or be more logical? There is a lot to be said for trusting your gut instinct and intuition, especially when your rational side doesn't have all of the facts and figures. Your heart is your emotion speaking and is easily coloured by circumstance, mood, history, and plenty of other things besides. Even if you're heart/emotion is telling you to make a decision one way always stop before you commit to it and ask yourself "Is this the *right* thing to do?"

'Right' needs some definition. Right for whom? Your business; you personally; the customer? You'll need to make a judgement call, but it is about trying to look at a situation objectively and ask, 'what would an impartial observer think is right'?

Then, do the right thing, even if it goes against your emotions.

6. Fight distractions and procrastination

In '60 Ways to Hurray!' I walk the reader through the FEDAMP Productivity Model so they can become a productivity ninja. The 'D' in FEDAMP stands for distraction, and there's a whole chapter devoted to trying to eliminate, or at the very least, minimise distractions. Why? Because these distractions are hell-bent on stopping your focus on achieving what needs to get done. These distractions are so tempting – which is why they are so dangerous. When you're under pressure, stressed, or maybe a bit bored, these distractions are fantastic (or so your brain tells you).

I also talk a lot about Focus and Action as two other parts of the model and the things that will push procrastination to one side. One of the sections is around the dangerous illusion that is 'perfection'. Perfection doesn't exist and waiting on it is just a significant procrastination enabler.

All these things are driven by emotion...feeling bored, feeling in want of some social media entertainment, feeling like you can't get started for any number of reasons. Sometimes you just don't feel like doing anything. But that's not an option if you want to achieve something, so you'll need to fight hard against it.

7. Trust intuition

Having said that you need to be detached and do the right thing above, there are times when it pays to trust intuition. Intuition may be influenced by emotion but is primarily defined by experience, the facts and figures at your disposal even if they are partial, the non-verbal cues received from people, and more besides. As you progress in your pursuit of goal achievement, you'll be guided by intuition and can evaluate how right it has been. This helps for the next time. Intuition is your subconscious, giving you a steer.

Trust it. Evaluate what happened. Modify for next time.

Solution Focus

A former peer at one company became a friend. We both left on the same day due to a large round of redundancies in the US and Europe. We both had running and sailing in common anyway, but then suddenly had the aftermath of a sudden release from gainful employment to deal with. We both needed to find a job.

He was very calm and clinical about it and took action right away. While I was still in shock with all sorts of self-doubting thoughts running through my head, he was on the phone to a recruiter. A couple of months later he was in a new role, happy that most of his pay-off was still in the bank, he had a great new job to get his teeth stuck into. I decided to go out and set up as a consultant to discover what that entailed, experiencing the freedom of the freelancer who isn't tied to one corporate.

It always struck me just how calm and unemotional he was about it all. I asked him how he managed to be like that. He told me that he just focused on the solution. The task was to find another job fast. And that's what he spent his time focusing on.

He is, in comparison to me, very unemotional. Knowing him as I do, there is emotion bubbling under the surface. It's just he's much better at keeping it at bay than I used to be.

Why? Because he focuses relentlessly on the solution.

If there's a problem, he's not interested in how the problem arose until after it is fixed. There's a large part of me that wants to know immediately how we got to this sorry state. He bypasses that, looking at what needs to be done to fix it.

I worked with him on a huge deal. A customer didn't like us at all. They had recommended to their board that they contract with an alternative vendor. We struggled to get traction with their senior team. My colleague and I were set the task of keeping the customer AND growing the revenue by a considerable amount.

I looked at everything from a million angles and saw all the potential and downsides, the what-ifs, and challenges. He looked at each piece in that puzzle and plotted how to solve the problems. His focus was laser-sharp on what the customer needed, what the specific individuals were looking for, and what our business objectives were. He spent no time dwelling on the potential issues, but all his time focused on the incremental steps to get to the desired end result, a result that would be beneficial to all parties.

As the negotiations progressed, there were many times when it seemed there was an insurmountable impasse. He would look at it and think 'what's the solution to this one?'. He'd go back with a compromise and a well-reasoned argument for why this would be in everyone's interests.

Even if he had self-doubts during the process, he never showed them. What he did show was a relentless focus on the solution. After only three months, we signed a brand-new contract worth many millions over a long duration, including a full technology refresh. Mission accomplished.

We're not all built in the same way. He either finds it easy to keep emotions in check or has become very practised at it. What is evident is that he is successful and calm in the way he manages his teams and business priorities.

When presented with challenges that I can get a bit emotional about, I always ask myself 'what would he do?'. And then I set about focusing on the solution, relentlessly driving to find it and achieve what needs to be done.

Always focus on the solution and not the problem. The solution is where you will find success.

The Mental Toughness Top 10

Self-discipline is essential, but it's not the same as discipline.

A combination of things achieves discipline:

1. Setting your goals
2. Knowing what you need to achieve to hit them
3. Ensuring you have a plan and give time to do them
4. Visualising the outcome of tasks and the ultimate goal
5. Celebrating success each time you achieve a little milestone
6. Forming habits so that tasks become part of the routine
7. Keeping your self-discipline in check

Discipline is a crucial component of being mentally tough.

Mentally tough people know what they want, they know their boundaries, and they summon the resolve to carry on in spite of setback, difficulty, tiredness, negativity, and other forces. There are several things they do, which set them apart from the average person.

If you want to develop your mental toughness, here are some of the things you should do every day until they become a habit. The more you practise something, the more it becomes part of who you are.

Creating positive habits is the surest way to become a better person. Creating these 'Mental Toughness' habits will help you to become a much stronger person.

1. **Always state goals in the positive.** Never run away from things; always run towards something. Always think in terms of what you want and not what you don't want. Always focus on what other people do to be successful and robust and emulate those behaviours, rather than focus on the things that you don't do which are holding you back. Always be positive. About everything. Always.

2. **Focus on the future and not the past.** We've all had difficult situations in our histories; arguments, job losses, relationship breakdowns, bereavements, horrible bosses. We've all made bad decisions; that 80s perm, the extra shot of vodka, that disastrous boyfriend/girlfriend, to work for a company that you thought was one thing but turned out to be another, to answer back to the headteacher. It isn't the past that defines us; it's the decisions we make about the future - what we want, what we do to get there, our attitude and actions. Focus on the future and leave the past behind, because people who dwell on the past often get stuck there.

3. **Learn from your mistakes.** Don't just repeat them over and over again. I said to focus on the future and not the past, but it will serve you well to take the learning points from the things that didn't go well and then apply them. Mentally strong people take responsibility for their actions, decisions and mistakes and put in place a plan to avoid making the same ones in the future. Writing things down helps to solidify the plan in your mind, as well as being evidence

of the commitment you're making, so put pen to paper and avoid the same mistakes again.

4. **Expect results to take time.** Expect that you'll need to put time and effort into getting to your desired goal. You've set yourself a goal that's no doubt challenging; you want to build a business, write a book, learn to fly a helicopter, win the local football Sunday league, run 5K without stopping. These require action over time. You don't get to take possession of your private helicopter's license without investing tens of thousands of pounds and hundreds of hours of land and air-based training. You can easily set up a business, but it will take time before it's successful and paying a healthy income. Writing a book requires hour upon hour of sitting on your own in a small room researching and typing hundreds of thousands of words, a considerable proportion of which will never make it into the book. To go from a couch potato to running 5K will take weeks of sustained effort. To win the Sunday league will never happen if everyone turns up with a hangover week in and week out. People who aren't mentally tough get distracted, bored and impatient, wanting results immediately. Change, development, learning and any goal worth chasing take time to achieve.

5. **Focus on the things you can control.** Can you control the weather? Or what other people think about you? Or the economy? Or every aspect of every little thing related to your goals? You can't control many things, and you certainly can't control everything. When I'm yacht racing, I can't control the weather or the tide, but I can control the choice of sail, the course to steer and the tactics employed to get off the line as close to the start gun as possible. You can't

possibly have everything under control - customers sometimes decide to cancel orders, the government raises taxes, cars break down, planes and trains are delayed, rivers flood, your boss decides they need something urgently, Tesco runs out of 'buy three for the price of two' offers on your favourite booze before the Hen Party pre-warm up. So, what can you control? Mentally tough people focus on the things that they can control and ignore everything else. Letting go of things you can't control will reduce anxiety and make you happier. You'll have more energy and less stress. Always think, "What are the things I can control?" and then act on them. The rest is in the lap of the gods.

6. **Keep on going.** It's easy to give some things up, especially when they are hard, or they've failed. You try, but it doesn't work. Maybe you try once more to see if, this time, it will. But it doesn't. You may think if it's failed twice it's unlikely to succeed, so give up. It's easy to understand the psychology of it because making a deliberate decision to give up feels much better than repeated failures. Your ego doesn't need to be dented any more. But mentally tough people keep on going - they don't give up. I used to sell fragrances door to door. Now that was a hard job full of failure and rejection, all day, every day. All I did to keep myself going was to look at the sales statistics of others doing the same job and realise that someone bought a perfume for every 30 interactions. Handling failure became easy because everyone that said 'No' was moving me closer to the (statistical) 30th. It was a case of 'So what? Next!'. And the thing I came to realise was that *I* hadn't failed when someone said no. It wasn't about *me* failing. It was about them not having any money, not wanting any perfume, being

too busy, having a bad day, or countless other things that I could not control. I had my goal to sell a set number of bottles a day, so I needed to talk to enough people to fill my quota.

7. **Accept the inequality of life.** Nobody owes you anything. Not a job. Not happiness. Not money. Nothing. You are not entitled to have a fancy car or a large house. You and I are a collection of cells that is no different from any other group of cells trying to live their lives. If you do have a nice car, or a great job, went to the best school, have money, or are deeply satisfied with life then you are lucky. Lucky to have been born into a family that cared for you. Lucky enough to have been born in a country with jobs on offer, or food available, or clean water, or no civil war. I didn't plan to be born in the UK to two amazing parents who put my siblings and me first, giving us every opportunity. I didn't plan to be a musician, or writer, or sailor or sales director. I was lucky to have been afforded the chance to learn to do those things. But I've also been unlucky, too. I've had businesses that didn't work. I was ripped off by a business partner to the tune of thousands of pounds when I was in my 20s. I didn't get every job I ever went for. Not every prospect bought something from me. Others are much more successful in business than I am. Others who earn a lot more. Many who are better sailors, musicians and writers. Some of them seem to have had more luck than me.

I could easily sit here and say that 'Life's not fair'. And I'd be right. It isn't. And it isn't meant to be. **Nobody owes me anything** - it is up to me to create my own luck and to drive towards my goals. Being mentally tough means being able to accept that life is not fair and focusing your efforts on getting to the goals you set for yourself. Realising this means that keeping score and comparing your achievements to others is a pointless and energy-sapping activity. We are all lucky, but some are luckier in some areas of their lives than we are. Focus on what you are doing and accept that nothing in life is fair.

8. **Keep your power.** If you've ever been in a situation where you've wanted to do something one way and then found that you're told to do it another, or that you've set a goal and changed it because others wanted you to do something else, then you've effectively given your power to someone else. You've put them in control of your goal, actions and success. When setting goals, write them down, define the process steps, measure progress, refine and keep driving forwards, even in the face of failure or set back. If you're clear enough about what you want to achieve and why then it'll help to make sure you don't inadvertently give your power to someone else.

9. **Take calculated risks.** Get comfortable with taking calculated risks because if you don't, you're unlikely to achieve any significant goals. Most goals necessitate a change of some description. To climb Everest means to get fitter, train for the freezing conditions, prepare for the worst and learn survival skills. To set up a new business is about changing lifestyle, work-life balance, swapping bosses, learning about ALL aspects of a business. While many goals require a change of some sort, many of these need you to take calculated risks. Is going to the top of Everest a risky thing to do? Is swapping the security blanket of a regular salary for the freedom of being the proprietor of your own business a risk? Risks can only be calculated if

there is knowledge about the threat. Mentally strong people seek knowledge and then make an assessment of the risk versus reward and whether there are alternative ways of achieving the end goal.

10. **Celebrate and learn from others' successes.** Life would be pretty dull if we were all equally good at everything. That some other people are more successful than us at some things is fantastic, because it shows us two things: 1) that success and improvement can be achieved, and 2) there's a blueprint from which to learn. The worst thing to do when beaten or we don't reach our aims is to feel sorry for ourselves. Wallowing in self-pity or beating yourself up is a harmful and highly destructive act. Mentally tough people don't see a failure to reach the bar as a negative. Instead, they see it is a learning opportunity. Look at how others did it. What can you do differently? What did it take for them to run a sub-4-hour marathon? Can you train as they did, or eat better, or change your mindset? To get a promotion, what did your colleague do, and how did they do it? To be the successful business owner, what did they learn, sacrifice, do or not do, how did they go about it, what was the timing of their growth plan, how did they handle risk and cash-flow? To achieve anything requires so much more effort than any of us can usually see on the surface, so we should applaud and celebrate others' success. Be happy that other people have 'made it' (whatever 'it' is) and learn 'how' they did it.

9. THE POWER OF THE TEAM

Get a Coach and Mentor

Depending on which side of the Atlantic you live will determine what you understand the words Coach and Mentor to mean. The saying that the 'United States and Great Britain are two countries separated by a common language' is widely attributed to George Bernard Shaw around the early 1940s. In the case of Mentoring and Coaching, this has never been truer.

In the US:

Mentoring - facilitating the mentee to their own solution without offering a solution or opinion
Coaching - offering specific advice about how to manage a task or issue

In the UK:

Mentoring - offering specific advice about how to manage a task or issue
Coaching - facilitating the coachee to their own solution without offering a solution or opinion

Confusing, huh? Rather than get hung up on the differences, let's focus on the two types of relationship/interaction and what benefits they can bring.

I don't much mind what each is called, or that there are 'distinct' differences listed in many articles and books about these two approaches. In fact, rather than be wedded to them as two separate things, see if you can find someone to provide you with support, guidance and help. In this chapter, I will use the terms mentor and coach interchangeably — it is in the specific relationship and contract you have between you, which determines if it is coaching or mentoring. Whatever it is, grasp the opportunity to learn from the experience of others. It is a gift — a precious one.

When Sir Richard Branson was setting up Virgin Atlantic, his mentor was Sir Freddie Laker. He said he wouldn't have got anywhere in the airline industry without the mentorship of Sir Freddie. The importance of having someone to look up to, who had the experience and could advise and inspire was invaluable to him. Laker Airways failed, but did that diminish the impact Sir Freddie had on Sir Richard? Not a bit. Being a mentor or coach is about using experience, both good and bad, to enable the recipient to find different solutions, ways of working, or business models. The importance of having a mentor is so powerful that the Virgin Group started a programme in 2013 with the Start-Up Loans Company to provide mentoring/coaching to entrepreneurs. I am a mentor with Virgin StartUp (the joint initiative), and it's incredible to see how having a mentor/coach helps keep the entrepreneurs on track, positive and feeling supported. For a variety of reasons, many start-ups fail, but through his experience with his own businesses, Sir Richard has put down a marker to make sure the reason for failure is not a lack of support or guidance in those early years.

When I was running my consulting business, I had many coaching clients. It was probably one of the most rewarding parts of my job. Not only can coaching and mentoring be invaluable for the receiver but for the coach/mentor, it is tremendously satisfying. That is why I'd recommend you not only find yourself a coach/mentor to help you develop your ideas and achieve your goals, but also become one to someone else. You will learn and grow through the act of giving.

So, just what are the benefits of coaching and mentoring?

A report published by ICF in 2009 showed that 80% of people who receive some coaching have an increased level of self-confidence, while there is an improvement in performance for 70%. And what about the cost-benefit analysis if you have to pay for coaching? The same report showed that 86% of companies stated they had made a positive return on their coaching investment. Those statistics are brilliant. People feel better, perform better, and it returns more to the bottom line.

My advice — get and be a mentor/coach. The rewards are real, educational, engaging, uplifting and tangible.

Spend 100% time with positive people

There's much evidence that positive thinking is good for us. From studies showing that people with a higher propensity to positive thoughts have a better immune function, an increased lifespan, are more resilient when life throws its little (or large) knocks and suffer from reduced stress. Being positive is a much more pleasant place to be, for you and those around you.

It's really easy to be cynical about things. That meal you just enjoyed with your significant other was great, but the service let it down a bit, and the wine wasn't as cold as it should have been. Or the film everyone is raving about has a few plot holes that don't quite add up while the acting was a little wooden from the third dragon on the left in scene 4. You can easily find fault in almost anything. But who wants to live in a world where the good is poisoned by the little things that weren't perfect? That's a dark and depressing place to live. It's terrible for your mental health, and if you want to achieve something great, you're going to have to suspend your disbelief and get more positive. In '60 Ways to Hurray!' I talk about how perfection is a harmful illusion. It doesn't exist. If you spend your time focusing on the things that aren't right, you'll be trapped in a procrastination loop that'll leave you feeling depressed and isolated.

You'll be the person that others joke about as the one who always finds something to complain about. How you're the one who manages to be a mood hoover and spoil something good with your laser focus on the things you didn't like.

Don't be that person. Be positive and look for the positive in everything. It'll help you mentally and emotionally and will help you achieve your goals.

While we're getting you more positive, let's run through the list of friends and acquaintances like you run through your wardrobe every season putting some out to the charity shop. Anyone who saps your energy, who sucks the fun out of life, or is cynical about what you're trying to do should be relegated to the 3rd team. If they continue in this way, bench them. Eventually, you may find you don't renew their pass into the ground.

I had a friend who couldn't resist being on a permanent downer. Everything I enthusiastically talked about wouldn't work, or there were issues, or he didn't believe could be done. I remember having a conversation with him about how one day people aren't going to watch films and TV programmes on their TV anymore at the prescribed times set by the television companies. 'That's rubbish,' he snorted. 'Why would anyone watch something on a smaller screen? People want to see things in their living room on a large screen. It'll never be the case.' He wasn't even prepared to discuss how or why people might watch on their iPhone or iPad. His mind was closed because he was in a permanent state of negativity. No matter what I suggested, he'd instantly be negative and find a reason it couldn't be the case.

I can't be dealing with that level of negativity or close-mindedness.

I'm not saying I only want 'yes-men' (equally yes-women) around me. I value constructive discussion and debate from many people so that ideas can evolve. This is healthy and a very good thing. I admit I may not always like the constructive feedback, but when it is 'constructive', it is very valuable.

Surround yourself with positive and constructive people – like-minded people who are looking to achieve the same sorts of amazing things you are.

And put those negative souls out with the bins on a Sunday night so they can be recycled somewhere else.

Eliminate the Negative

Did you know that productivity has been shown to decrease by up to 18% when people lose interest and passion in their work and that one of the things which can contribute to this is a negative work environment? It stands to reason that if there's a negative atmosphere at work, it'll have a negative impact on your mood. You know those mood hoovers? Those people who in a matter of minutes leave you feeling depressed? One moment you're feeling good, and then someone says something negative about what you've done or are wanting to do, your work or something personal, and the next moment you feel deflated.

Of course, we are all calibrated differently. For some people, a negative comment here or there will hardly register, but for others, it makes a reasonably quick impression. Even those who have thicker skin will eventually be affected. Imagine a negative atmosphere in which to work. That'd make most of us feel a little less like going the extra mile or being as productive as possible.

In a negative work environment studies show that absenteeism is higher, workers are less engaged, there are more accidents, and people make more mistakes. People can be fearful, and there is likely to be a higher attrition rate which costs tens of thousands of pounds to remedy, not to mention the time, effort and energy that needs to be spent on on-boarding a new starter.

Some of the factors negatively impacting the workplace include toxic management — where the manager may bully or withhold information, may show favouritism or take credit for team members' work — or workplace gossiping — where the negative tittle-tattle about others makes you wonder what they're saying about you. Several studies have shown that those two factors can lead to disengagement and increase the likelihood of leaving a business.

When people are positive and engaged with their workplace/employer, the business can make up to 26% more profit per employee according to one survey. Think of the corollary to that; every employee who is not engaged only generates 3/4 of the potential profit made by those at a company that is seen as a 'great place to work'.

If a negative workplace can have a materially adverse impact on the employees and the business, it's a short jump to suggest that any negative influences on you are likely to have a pretty significant detrimental effect on your chances.

Take action today and eliminate anything negative from your work environment. In fact, go one better and try to remove harmful or toxic things or people from your life. You will not regret it at all. You will feel lighter, happier, healthier.

Bin the negative and fill the void with as much positivity as you can. You will never regret making this one change.

Network, network, network

I read a book by Keith Ferrazzi called 'Never Eat Alone'. It was first published in 2014 and is worth a read. He networks brilliantly, engaging with people on a personal level.

When I was a young sales guy, I remember my sales director 'encouraging' me to get out and about with customers. 'You don't build relationships or sell anything sitting in the office. Get out and spend as much time as you can with your customer.' He was quite formidable when he was cross, and he was cross with me. I made a point of booking some breakfast meetings with clients the next day. I arranged drinks with another one. And then lunch. My expenses went through the roof, but nobody seemed to mind much back at the office. My relationships with customers improved, and we started to get more business. Cause and effect? I reckon so.

Leaving the safety of paid work and setting up as an independent consultant was daunting. How do I go about finding new business? Who's going to buy from me? The answer — no-one if they didn't know I was out consulting. The consultancy I was working with used to talk about 'coffee to cash' meetings. It's the same principle as 'never eat alone'. I set up a load of coffees, lunches, drinks, and dinners with everyone who I'd ever had an acquaintance with. It was great fun, learning about them, reconnecting, looking for ways I could help them. Meeting after meeting of interesting stuff went past. Then one person saw an opening for me to help. I ended up doing a series of jobs for them over the course of a year. I made sure I bought this contact lunch a few more times. He recommended I speak to someone else and put in a good word for me. I purchased the new contact a coffee too.

Whenever I need to eat, I now wonder who I can take with me. Eating alone isn't much fun. Laughing, chatting, sharing a bottle of wine with someone else is.

Another key lesson from Keith Ferrazzi is to 'never keep score'. Many of us tend to think about things in terms of a quid pro quo — *'if I do something nice for you, I expect something nice in return'*. 99% of the time, you'll get nothing back. You need to reframe your mindset. Keith's advice is sound – don't keep a scorecard. Instead, see every kind act as an investment in your future, but not necessarily a future with that specific person. Imagine how quickly you'd stop doing things for others if every time you didn't get anything back in return, you felt aggrieved.

You had dinner with a busy person who gave you their time. You may have bought it, but they gave you their precious and valuable time. You learned stuff from them. You enjoyed a joke or two and had some delicious food. Now tell me you didn't get anything in return.

One of the most important things to remember when building relationships and networking is to be genuine. It's easy to spot a fake, only interested in you for their own aims. These people mostly talk about themselves, pitch to you, and drop you quickly when someone more interesting, or useful, comes along. Fakes are easy to see through. Don't be one of them.

Instead, be more interested than interesting. Learn something about them and be genuinely interested in them. Ask more questions, let them tell their stories and look for ways to make them feel good or help. Always follow up with them afterwards.

Maya Angelou said, *'I've learned that people will forget what you said, people will forget what you did, but people will never forget how you made them feel.'* Send them a hand-written card afterwards, not an email. Hand-written cards feel personal and take time and effort to write. You will be remembered for your gesture long after the fakes are forgotten.

Make them feel good by giving a gift at an unexpected moment. I've just read a great book called 'Giftology' by John Ruhlin, published in 2018. He tells of the power of gifting to build relationships that last. His is the ultimate guide to networking and maintaining meaningful relationships.

How to Network Effectively

Some people love networking. Some people are just really sociable and find talking to strangers easy. Some can happily socialise all day long. I am not one of them. If I don't have enough quiet time to collect my own thoughts and recharge my batteries, I feel really off balance. I'm quite happy to talk to anyone, but too much of it and my energy is depleted rapidly.

You know those corporate events where you get talked at for two days? Senior management and functional departments update you on the year to date or new initiatives for service or operational improvement. Sales management rev up the sales teams in January for the year ahead "Last year was fantastic, but this year it's going to be the best on record". Competitions for places in the coveted Challenger Club (other names are available) of top salespeople who win an all-expenses-paid trip to some far-flung location with their partners and colleagues for 4-5 days.

These corporate events are important. Without them, no one would know what's going on, and relationships wouldn't be built. All the companies I've worked for run on relationships. They have processes and tools, but mostly, these aren't very efficient. If I need to get a sales order booked and pushed through to delivery, it's the strength of my relationship with that team that will make the difference. And the best place to build those relationships is at these events.

For most people, these events are a great fun excuse to get out of the office, to learn something about the company strategy, get inspired, be part of the bigger picture and feel valued. Most importantly, they're an opportunity to socialise and drink a little too much.

Networking is one of the most essential skills to master if you're going to accelerate your performance in any field. Think about something you want to achieve, do you think you're more likely to achieve it if you work with others, get feedback, coaching, introductions to others, encouragement, or anything else from those around you?

To network effectively, you need to consider five things:

1. **Preparation** - what is it you're trying to achieve? What type of person is interesting for you to meet and exchange details with? What are you in need of? What is it you offer to others (it's not a one-way street)?

Whatever event you are going to, research others on the invitation list. Make your own list of those you want to target and get specific about who they are, their background, experience, and interests. Most people love to talk about themselves and what interests them, so find out as much as possible before the event and write it down.

Write down what you are looking for. Is it an introduction to a publisher, personal trainer, or the Chief Operating Officer to pitch your cost-saving idea? Is it for some coaching, or to learn from how they achieved something similar to your goal? Whatever it is, be specific.

Against each of your targets write down something you've done that relates to them or their interests/experiences. Have a think about what you could offer them. Look for the common ground. Write it down. Make a plan.

I've lost track of the number of events I've been to where I didn't make an effort to network effectively and missed an opportunity. I now wish I had their details so I could call and run something past them.

2. **Listen** - be more interested than interesting. This is so important. This isn't an opportunity for you to bore your new contact with everything you have to say. It's your opportunity to build rapport and establish some common ground. If you're nervous, resist the temptation to gabble at them. Instead, ask lots of questions and respond to them appropriately. It should be about you showing a genuine interest in what they have to say, what they do, what makes them tick, makes their company unique, what they like doing on the weekends.

We all have two ears and one mouth. We should use them in that proportion. Listen, Listen, Speak, Listen, Listen, Speak.

If you've done your research well before attending and are talking to one of your targets, quite a bit of what they tell you won't be news to you. Don't let on that you know it all otherwise you'll seem like a stalker. Listen intently and provide some insight or information of your own that complements what they've said.

If you're talking to someone who you've not researched or didn't intend to target you should still listen, intently. How do you know what they have to offer if you don't find out? And you can't find out unless you listen, actively building a conversation. Everyone deserves respect and time, so give it to them. Be interested and learn something. Be curious and find some common ground. If they are not ultimately helpful to your current goals, who's to say they may not be for future ones.

Stephen Covey said that most people listen not for the purpose of understanding but with the purpose of replying. If you're thinking about your reply while someone is speaking, you can't fully engage in what they are saying. Active listening is a skill that is in decline - we are all so busy updating our followers on InstaBook, FaceGram and Twitterers that we seem to be on permanent transmit mode. You can't listen when transmitting.

3. **Ask their advice** - everyone has an opinion, and many of those you meet at these events will have experience, contacts or insights that they'll be willing to share for free. Make them feel like you value them and ask them what they'd do if they were trying to achieve what you are. They may ask you a bunch of questions at this point, and it's OK to answer them and talk about yourself as by this stage you've already learned a lot about them.

At one event in Helsinki, I asked all my contacts how they would approach the market if they had technology like the one we were developing. Some answers were obvious, but some were gold nuggets, things we hadn't thought about ourselves. This open question, after I'd made them feel special and valued, provided us with some beneficial ideas about how to develop our go-to-market plans. I asked some of them, who I knew by this stage to be interested in hearing more if we could set up a more formal demo with our CEO. I asked some if they knew anyone who might be able to help us get some press coverage, and others whether we could think about some mutual trial to see whether each other's technology would benefit the other.

We got press coverage from it. We got some trial agreements signed. We gathered some excellent ideas to help us develop our plans further.

4. **Record** - Write the information you learn down. Straight away. Otherwise, you WILL forget it. Take their business card and add it to an app like Evernote by snapping a photo. Then add a few notes about your conversation. Don't have a phone with you? Then take their business card and scribble on the back of it. Consolidate all the information once you get back to base.

Segment the people you met into groups. Those who are super-hot. Those who were interesting. Those who you can't see any immediate reason to be in touch with. Those you liked personally. Some of these lists will intersect.

5. **Follow-up** - with everyone you meet. A quick personal two to three-line email is all it takes. Make it personal about something you discussed and, if applicable, include the agreed follow-up actions.

Connect with everyone on LinkedIn. That way, you can find them again easily.

For those you didn't particularly like or don't think can help you, send a quick note. Might they be useful one day?

For those you think are useful contacts add in something extra. Something personal. An article you've read that you think they'll enjoy. Or something about a book you read that they might like to read (usually best if it's relevant to the topic under discussion).

For those you struck a good rapport with, send a handwritten note to them as well as a short follow up email. Everyone likes receiving something other than a bill or flyer through the letterbox, and they'll remember you.

For those, you think you can strike up a good and mutually beneficial relationship with perhaps send them a book directly from Amazon with a gift note, instead of just telling them about it in an email or handwritten note.

It's all a matter of judgement. Don't be stalkerish about it.

And then follow up again. Buy them a coffee. Send them a text or email on their birthday. Be positive in each interaction and add value to them every time you are in contact. Give, give, give, and you'll get when the time is right.

Importantly, don't expect anything in return. Many (possibly most) won't reply. You may not even get a follow-up note or a thank you. That's OK. You're not doing this to have your ego massaged. You're doing this because when the time is right, and you need some support, you can ask for it and you're likely to get it.

Back in Helsinki, I made some contacts from networking who I am still connected to. I'm not in their industry any longer, but I bet you any money that if I needed some advice or an introduction, I'd get it if I asked. And, so would they.

Your network is your most potent and prized asset. Develop it with integrity. Maintain it with a genuine desire to learn and provide value to those in it. Don't be a leech sucking the life out of everyone you meet. No-one likes a leech.

A Reason, A Season, Or A Lifetime

Very few people in our lives are permanent. Most come in for some time and then disappear again, and even if they don't completely disappear, their significance changes. The continuous ever-presence of a parent, sibling or child. The colleagues with whom you share a relationship for a few years while you toil on behalf of a shared company goal. The school or university friends who you once couldn't live without but have not had any communication with for over 30 years. The wife or husband you pledged to love until death parts you, but whom you split from acrimoniously leaving the dog traumatised. The accountant who gave that specific piece of advice that you needed at just the right time. The person who popped up only when you were going through a really tough time, but you don't keep up with anymore.

You're grateful to them all. But all relationships are fluid, to a degree. It would be impossible to keep in touch with everyone we ever met. Social Media helps keep us in touch with many more people these days, but it can be so very superficial. Keeping up with all the people we've met and shared something with is nearly impossible.

There's a saying that people come into our lives for a reason, a season or a lifetime.

Just make sure you recognise the people who help you along the way. And be prepared to give something back when they need you. Networking with integrity involves getting and giving.

Two Way

Have you ever considered your relationships in terms of what they are bringing to you and what you are bringing to them?

It's essential to give as well as get but striving for that balance is hard. I don't know about you, but I have some contacts who never seem to want to give. It always seems to be about them. No matter how I might hope for something in return, it just never seems to be that important to them.

I'm not advocating that you stop your own generosity of spirit in going the extra mile for those who need it, but I am advocating being a little more ruthless about who you help when you have a goal to achieve that has a clear and defined purpose behind it. You need people around you who can complement and assist in that effort. Those who take without giving back sap your energy and deflect from your mission. Steer clear of the mood, time and energy hoovers.

On the flip side, if you have people willing to provide you with support, time, energy, and commitment, or are happy to have some tasks delegated to them, then you owe them. You need to think in terms of what you can do for them. First, because it's the right thing to do and second because the world works based on give-and-take. If you take, take, take then you will find yourself being the very same mood, time and energy hoover you're now trying to avoid.

Small Teams

If you want to know how to do something, it's a good idea to ask others who've done it before about it. What's their experience been? Did they overcome challenges, and if so, how? What was their strategy? What were the things that went really well? Find a few people with similar expertise who had different experiences. Pulling all of this together will allow you to short-circuit some decisions, to focus on the things that worked well for others and achieve your goal more efficiently.

Gathering collective experience together is invaluable. But is it always best to have lots of people involved in a project, meeting or team? Science says no. We've all had experiences of meetings with a large number of people. Half are disengaged, doing their admin or emails, a few are listening, while possibly only one or two are actively engaging. More often than not, there will be a dominant alpha-type who likes the sound of their own voice, proffering opinion and ideas.

The one thing that everyone will agree on afterwards is that the meeting didn't achieve much. The next time you're in a meeting like this try to work out how much the meeting has cost - guess everyone's salary, calculate the hourly rate per person, then multiple by the number of people and the hours wasted. Meetings are expensive!

Now think back to a meeting that you've held with just one other person, and you got something achieved. How long was the meeting? How much did it cost? Did you come out with a clear set of agreements or an action plan? I'd bet you that it was cheaper, faster and more productive. Why? Because with only two of you, you have no choice but to engage, to work through the agenda, and you have the opportunity to make decisions without others interfering.

Science can explain why large groups are bad for productivity and personal performance.

You've heard the expression 'herding cats', used about getting many people coordinated around a date, an idea, an activity or a set of objectives. There are three things main things which need managing, and the larger the number of people, the exponentially bigger the challenge becomes. You go from herding a few cats to hundreds of them in no time at all.

1. Coordinating the connections or relationships between people is the first of the three challenges. It's not just about how many people you have in the group, but the number of links or contact points.

    Imagine there are three other people in your team. That's four people with six connection points. How does that follow? Draw four points on a piece of paper as if they are the corners of a square. Now draw lines between them all. Six lines. That is manageable. Now take a group of ten people and connect all the ten dots. How many links are there? 45. A group of 60 people has *1,770* connection points to manage.

    Why does this matter? Because if you work in a large team, you've got a lot of people to keep informed of progress. A lot of people to coordinate and integrate. There is a considerable cost to making sure everyone knows what's happening, that they have a say, and buy into whatever is being worked on. Don't tell me you've not sat in a meeting with a host of other people and thought that only a fraction of the meeting was relevant to you, with the rest being about others 'getting up to speed', or ideas being 'socialised'. It's not for no reason that software teams work in small, agile scrum teams of just a few. Anywhere between four to nine people is considered good, with around six to seven being optimal. So next time you're thinking of working on a project, consider how many people are really needed. And, if your project is running late, seriously consider whether adding more people to it will not, in fact, make it a whole lot later. If you add more people, you have even more connections and people to 'get up to speed' and 'socialise' stuff with.

2. Have you ever seen people loafing in meetings or teams? Social loafers who aren't as motivated when in a group as they would if they were on their own. When people are part of a group, they become less productive and motivated. Simply by being part of a group! Bibb Latane, Kipling Williams and Stephen Harkins conducted a study in 1971 which placed people in groups. They were blindfolded and given noise-cancelling headphones. They were then asked to shout as loudly as they could. When in groups of six people, they used 36% of their full volume. Just 36%. Hardly as loud as they could be. And when this was controlled by placing people alone but telling them they were in groups, they still only shouted at 74% of their loudest.

When people are alone, they use their full voice.

Social loafing is about feedback in a group. As the group gets larger, there is less social pressure, and it becomes tough to assess your performance in a crowd correctly. People, therefore, put in less effort than they otherwise would if they were alone or in a smaller group. Another result of being in a larger team or group is that people start to feel more disconnected with the task and results. That isn't good for anyone's performance.

3. The last issue is that there is a relational loss. In January 2012, Jennifer Mueller wrote a piece entitled 'Why individuals in larger teams perform worse'. In it, she concludes that people feel relational loss when they think they're receiving less and less support, be it emotional, information, help or assistance. The result of relational loss can be feelings of isolation and stress, which lead to poorer performance than would have been evident had the team been much smaller. Keep the team smaller, and the feeling of isolation will diminish. Companies are always saying they want to empower their people, and now they can, by keeping groups small and focused.

Smaller teams perform better and feel better. Smaller teams are more engaged. They are more productive. And consequently, can accelerate the performance of the company.

10. ESSENTIAL TOOLS

Overcoming blocks

Sometimes I get stuck. I have ideas but can't progress them. The blog post I want to write seems like a mountain to climb. The idea of running a 5k park run is just too much. My dream of singing at the 606 club in London is just so 'out there' I'll never achieve it.

What's stopping me from doing all of these things? Assuming you have the physical ability, means and time to progress them, it is likely to be your own limiting beliefs that are getting in your way.

Your limiting beliefs are those that tell you "you can't do something because" … "that it won't work because" … "that it'll fail because" … it's those voices in the head that block your progress.

Here are some blockers and suggestions to help overcome them:

- If fear or doubt paralyse and stop you from moving forward, scale back the ambition into manageable bite-sized chunks. Then progress with each smaller step, step-by-step.
- Fear of failure can make it hard to start something. It's a debilitating feeling, and something I'll tell you a story about in the next section. The best way

to combat these feelings is to remind yourself of a time (or times) when you were successful, when something you did turned out well. Focus on the things that went right and where you achieved something to help you overcome this understandable inertia.

- You have a hunch it won't work, so you justify not doing anything by saying your gut is telling you it's not worth it. My advice — don't rely on your gut. Your gut tells you that you need to supersize your McDonald's when you're hungry. Your head knows it's not necessary; empty calories. You can't always trust your gut. You can seek out the facts and make a decision based on information. If your gut feeling is you can't do something check the facts and base your decision on the facts. If your head says the facts make sense, then go with it.

There are more potential limiting beliefs, but you get the idea. In the next section, we'll look at how to reframe your thoughts so that you can get over almost any blocks and grab what you're aiming to achieve.

Reframing

Our lives are a series of stories. Things that happen to us. Things we go out and do. Things with friends and family members. Talk to anyone, a stranger, and ask them to tell you the story of their life, and it will be fascinating. What influenced them? Who they grew up with? What were the key moments in their lives that changed their thinking or the course of events? Did they find love and lose it? Or find it and still have it today. Get them to tell their story and be awed, humbled or just plain interested, for half an hour or more.

This is why interviews in magazines of the kind of 'day in the life' get read, or why we tune into programmes like 'Life Stories'. To hear what happened to other people, how they reacted, coped, celebrated, or got over some tragedy. We are all nosy. Or should that be - interested?

It all depends on how you look at something; what perspective you take. What version of a story you choose to pay attention to?

When we tell stories, we tell a version from our own perspective, based on the memories we have and the interpretations we've made about a situation. If you ask two people to tell their story about an event they were both at, it's going to have differences. One person may see it as a positive, fun and informative event, the other as a boring waste of time — same event; different filter.

It begs the question about whether 'truth' really exists. One person's truth is another person's fiction, but that's a subject for a cleverer philosopher than me!

When you tell yourself a story, or you see something from your own perspective, note how it feels to you. Is it positive or negative? How easily could you change the feelings if you wanted to?

The answer is relatively easily. It all comes down to how you reframe your thinking.

Reframing is the ability to adapt your thoughts by putting a different frame around them — a picture with a metaphorical different frame. Great leaders and achievers can reframe their thinking to drive more positive outcomes.

We've talked about limiting beliefs and how it's possible to see past these and remove them so you can move forward. Reframing is the technique used to achieve this — see a different perspective and modify the way you feel and think about it.

You can use this technique for almost anything else. Earlier I said I'd tell my story as an example of reframing.

My first audition to gain entry to the Guildhall School of Music and Drama was in 1989. I was 18 and had been singing to a high standard in my Grade 8 – baritone solos for concerts, the jazz groups I was in and other ensembles. People seemed to enjoy what I was doing and commented on my voice being good.

I had no idea what else to do with life after school, and so I opted to carry on the family profession of music, specifically singing. I enrolled for auditions at the Guildhall. On the day itself, I was a bundle of nerves.

Oh, my God! The other singers warming up in the practice rooms around mine were sensational. I listened to one chap giving it large on an aria from Mozart and started getting heart palpitations. The girl in the room opposite was singing 'Vissi d'arte' from Tosca, beautifully. Holy Crap. I was so intimidated I convinced myself my quest was futile and that every nice, well-meaning person who'd ever paid me a compliment was a deluded lunatic. And as for my mum and dad, they'd thought my attempt at a 3D model of a castle made from egg boxes and toilet rolls was the best piece of art they'd ever seen so they clearly couldn't be trusted!!

I warmed up and sat on the row of chairs outside the audition room like I was on death row. I was so convinced I was going to be positively shit in comparison to everyone else. So much so that I had the demeanour of a broken boy.

I had a choice to make: 1) go through with it in the defeatist funk I was in, 2) leave and avoid the humiliation, or 3) reframe my thinking.

As a 16-year-old, I'd started getting fascinated by what these two American men were doing in the world of psychology. Richard Bandler and John Grinder had written some fascinating books like 'Turning Frogs into Princes', and I'd read them all. It had been in my 1st year A' Level that a man had come to the school looking for volunteers to help in his research for this thing called NLP (Neuro-Linguistic Programming). He sat me down, and I had to answer a whole load of music aural tests while being filmed. I'm confident I got every single one of them wrong, but he said that didn't matter. What he was studying were my eye movements as I answered. Apparently, depending on whether you are visualising or remembering something, your eyes go to different places. Who knew? Certainly not a spotty 16-year-old. It was fascinating, so I read a few books about it all.

One thing I was fascinated by was the concept of reframing. Taking a belief and changing it by reframing the way it was thought about. I forget which of their books it was in, but one story was about how a person with severe phobias related to spiders was effectively cured through the application of some reframing. Wow!

I was going to get me some of that. My fear of humiliation and defeat was not going to beat me.

As I sat on what felt like death row, I started to visualise my audition going well. I imagined the smiling faces of the audition panel. I saw the accompanist looking up at me from the music in astonishment as I filled the room with the best rendition they'd ever heard, of Peter Warlock's 'Ha'nacker Mill'.

I started to feel excited rather than petrified. I breathed deeply and slowly. I told myself 'I am a singer. I am a performer.' Over the space of about 15 minutes, I transformed from terrified, defeated, hunched imposter to a confident, tall, performer who had something to say. I had done my equivalent of the confidence pose before an interview, but I had done it in my head with the power of reframing.

I was accepted to the Guildhall aged 18 and was thrilled. Bravely, or stupidly, I declined my place and opted to work for a year so that my voice had a chance to mature before embarking on my studies. Was I mad? It wasn't even a deferral. I'd have to go through the same thing again one year later and compete against yet more amazingly brilliant singers to get a place. However, somehow, through reframing, I felt confident enough to go through it all again (my confidence helped by having been accepted once, though there were no guarantees a second time).

One year later, I auditioned and received an offer I gladly accepted. 'Ha'nacker Mill' served me well again that day.

The power of reframing is not to be underestimated. Whatever you think you know about a situation or story, there are always other ways of looking at them. Different perspectives. And it may just be that another view is more helpful than the one you have today.

If you want to excel at anything, or if you're going to accelerate your performance, practise the art of reframing so that the feelings you have towards whatever you're trying to achieve, serve you best.

Neuro-Linguistic Programming

I've mentioned NLP a few times in this book. It is the most brilliant thing, and I'd encourage you to seek out a book or two to become more familiar with what it is and what it can offer. It's a subject covered by people better qualified to write about it than me, so rather than do the matter a disservice I will recommend a few books to look out for. It's not for everyone, but it is something I would strongly recommend investigating. It has been transformative for me.

My recommended books are:

- ✓ **Frogs into Princes** by Richard Bandler & John Grinder (the founders of NLP) - this is only available second-hand
- ✓ **Using Your Brain for a Change** by Richard Bandler - this is only available second-hand
- ✓ **Neuro-linguistic Programming for Dummies** by Romilla Ready
- ✓ **NLP Workbook: A Practical Guide to Achieving the Results You Want** by Joseph O'Connor (he's the chap who used me in his research in 1988 and who sparked my interest in NLP)
- ✓ **Introducing NLP** by Joseph O'Connor

11. CAN YOU DO ME A FAVOUR?

If you've enjoyed this book and it's helped you in some way please can you do me a favour and write a review on Amazon?

If you do you'll be helping accelerate the book's performance as well as enabling loads of other people to benefit.

Please visit:

http://accelerate-performance.com/feedbackAPP

and then leave a review on the Accelerate Performance website or go to Amazon and leave one there. If you're feeling amazingly generous, how about both? I'd be enormously grateful.

Thank you very much in advance.

12. MORE AT ACCELERATE-PERFORMANCE.COM

You might have bought this book because you found the Accelerate Performance website first. Or you might have found us from Amazon, or elsewhere.

Wherever you stumbled upon this book remember there are lots of articles, tips and tricks on the Accelerate Performance website.

Find us at accelerate-performance.com

If you have any comments or extra ideas to make this book even better, or that will add to the 67 ideas in "60 Ways to Hurray!", then let me know.

You can email me at info@accelerate-performance. com or leave feedback at:

http://accelerate-performance.com/feedbackAPP

Thank you for buying and virtual hugs for reading.

ABOUT THE AUTHOR

Ralph Varcoe is an author, musician, and highly experienced business leader who has spent way too many years building businesses and teams.

From taking a mail order book business to being a publisher while still at college, creating an online community and social network for the boating community, working as a consultant in multiple technology companies, driving sales and marketing growth through Europe and beyond, building sales strategies and teams to deliver value to customers globally, to acting as a business mentor for entrepreneurs and start-ups, Ralph has a wealth of experience in what it takes to perform at the top level, and guide others to do the same.

He is a trained singer, having performed classical and jazz at venues from London to Shanghai, and writes and records songs for fun. He is an avid sailor, having skippered his team to 1st place in a number of regattas, and is passionate about giving women a greater and more valued position in the working world. He has a partner, with four daughters between them, and lives in Hampshire, UK.

Printed in Great
Britain
by Amazon